Boxes to Build

Boxes to Build

Sturdy & Stylish Projects to Organize Your Home & Shop

From the Editors of Popular Woodworking

CEDAR LANE PRESS

Page 126

CONTENTS

Page 14

1. SMALL BOXES

2. CHESTS & STORAGE

3. CABINETS

Page 51

1 SMALL BOXES

SMALL BOXES MAKE FANTASTIC GIFTS, and are a great way to utilize shorter pieces of stock you may have been saving up in your shop. Everyone can use a little more organization—the clever boxes showcased here will become dedicated spots for whatever you need, be it a caddy for tools or arts and crafts materials, or a delicate receptacle for jewelry, trinkets, spare change, or even photographs and keepsakes. And let's not forget that so many woodworking pieces begin with the humble shape of an enclosed box, including birdhouses. The projects feature decorative and practical details like dovetail joinery, bent wood, sliding lids, inlay, and more.

Ashtastic. This ash, finger-jointed jewelry box is simple to build with just a few tools: A bandsaw, chisel, handplane, and router are all that's required.

JASMINE JEWELRY BOX

Simple tools, techniques & joinery deliver elegant results.

BY GARY ROGOWSKI

It's the stuff of arguments: Which tools in the shop are really the most important for joinery? It's almost like arguing the top movie or the best shortstop of all time. There is no one answer that satisfies everyone (although "The Maltese Falcon" and "Ernie Banks" should). Were you to ask me, my answers would be quick but not absolute. Give me three tools—a bandsaw, a chisel, and a router—and I can build just about anything. This jewelry box project shows how versatile these tools are.

Divisible by three. To lay out your finger joints, place a ruler at the edge of your board, then angle it to the opposite edge until you have a measurement easily divisible by three—and ensure the center slot is a hair wider than the chisel you wish to use.

Tight shims. You must use shims that fit tightly into your saw kerfs. If you don't have veneer that will serve, cut shims at the bandsaw.

Notch test. With stock at the ready, sized the same in width as your actual pieces, set your bandsaw fence to make the first cut for the center notch, then flip the board and cut the second side of the notch. Make sure your shims fit the slots tightly and check that your chisel will fit just inside the waste.

Fit test. To cut the matching part of the joint, slip the end of the shim between the fence and your stock, and make the cut with the shimmed stock held tight to the fence, then flip the board and make the second cut.

Choose your joinery on three factors: function, economy, and skill. What will the piece do? This poses the question: How strong does it need to be? There are 10 ways of building this box and all of them are good. But which one of these methods is strong enough and adds something to the design?

How quickly does it need to be made? Is this jewelry box a diversion or a Christmas or birthday present? If it's the latter, then almost by definition it's late. The speed at which you work will come into play. You might want to use dovetail joints, but you don't have the time to handcut them. But you can quickly cut a finger joint that looks pretty good using the bandsaw.

Finally, what are you capable of doing in your shop with your tools and your skills? You might want something a lot prettier than a butt joint and you have the tools and time to do it. This finger-jointed box offers in its design strength, simplicity, and symmetry in equal measures.

FINGER JOINTS ON THE BANDSAW

To lay out the finger joints, I divided the width of the box side into thirds. Take a ruler and put the corner of it at one edge of the board and rotate the ruler until it hits the other edge at a number easily divisible by three. Mark out your thirds and square those marks out to the end of the board. Just make certain that the width of the center slot is a hair wider than one of your chisels. This way your chisel will enter more easily when chopping out the waste. For this box measuring 2¼" high, I used a ¾" chisel and the remaining space divided up at ¾" evenly. This is not critical for the strength. What is critical is how accurately you set up to cut these joints. Before beginning this method, try out this bandsaw technique on a piece of scrap. First, all your stock has to be the same width. Triple check and adjust as needed. Next, you'll need to make a shim that fits the width of the cut that your blade makes. This kerf will vary from blade to blade, so make a practice cut in a board and try to find a shim that fits well. Perhaps two pieces of veneer glued together will work. Maybe you'll need to add a piece of masking tape to them to increase the thickness—or shave or scrape a little off the veneer instead to thin it. You may have to make your own shim by cutting it on the bandsaw. But however you make this shim, it has to fit the kerf tightly or the joint won't fit.

Use a bandsaw blade with at least 4 to 6 teeth per inch to cut the joint. Cut the center notch first. Set up your fence distance to cut the closer of the two side walls of this notch. Line it up to make a notch wide enough for your chisel and make sure to mark the baseline for your cuts on this test board at slightly less than the board's thickness. Make the first cut up to this line. Flip the board and make the matching cut on this slot. Mark this slot as waste, then check that the shim fits tightly. Adjust the shim as needed.

For the matching cut, nothing changes on the bandsaw except that you introduce the shim between the fence and the second board. Keep that board tight to the fence as you make the cuts and keep the shim always close to the end that's being cut. What's happening, of course, is that the second board is being pushed away from the fence by the width of the cut. If your shim is too loose, then so will be your joint. If it's too tight in the kerf, then you'll have trouble closing the joint. You can see this relationship when you hold the two boards up to one another. Once you cut away the waste, the joint should just fit snugly together with hand pressure.

End-to-end match. If your cuts are set up and shimmed correctly, the inside edges of your kerfs should align.

Ease the edges. Use a block plane to chamfer the ends of your stock now, before you make any cuts.

JOINERY DETAILS & FITTING

One of the important ways to set a project apart is to detail it. With these finger joints, I make them protrude through and chamfer their ends to call them out. Set up your marking gauge for the thickness of the stock plus 1⁄32" to 1⁄16" more. Have your center slot marked out on the two long boards and mark their faces. For the end boards with the single finger in the middle, mark out the faces and the edges of the board. Next, chamfer the ends of your boards with a block plane. Using your block plane again (or a sander), clean up the ends of your boards. It will be simpler with less risk of tear out to do all this work now rather than later.

With your shim the perfect size, cut out the four notches on your long boards. A simple precaution when cutting is to set up a stop on the fence to prevent going past the gauge line. Cut these center slots first, mark out the waste sections, then add the shim and make the matching cuts on the shorter boards. Mark out the waste pieces on their ends too.

Use a narrow bandsaw blade to remove the waste more easily in the center slot. (If all you have is a wide blade, make a series of cuts to remove it.) When you get close to the line, with a deft touch, you can nibble away the waste by moving side to side, just catching the teeth. Get as close as you can to the line then chop out the waste with your chisel. Once you get started with your cuts, you can undercut the end grain a little to make the job go faster.

Before removing the waste on the ends, start to chop out the waste on your end slots about 1⁄16" to 1⁄8" deep. Chop down from both the faces and the edges of your boards to establish the plane of the end sockets. It's easier to get these cuts established now, then bandsaw off the waste close to the gauge lines. You can pare these end sockets flat later for a great fit. Just be sure not to chop down too hard or your chisel will be forced off the gauge line and into the good wood. This can be visible from the edges.

After chopping, clean up the box sides with a handplane and scraper to remove any working marks.

ROUTING FOR THE BOTTOM

After fitting the joints, I lay out and cut the grooves for the bottom at my router table. I line a piece of plywood with a decorative paper for this jewelry box, so I make the bottom from 1⁄4" plywood (which, of course, measures something less than that). Check how thick your paper makes your plywood package before routing the grooves. Set the fence at the proper distance from the bit and set the bit height for two cuts at 3⁄32" or one at 3⁄16".

Stopped cuts are used on the longer pieces, so I set stops on my fence to limit the travel distance of the cut. To find where the bit starts cutting, simply hold a block to the bit, rotate the bit backward by hand and mark on the fence where the block stops moving. This will be one cutting edge of the bit. Do the same for the other side. With stop marks penciled on the top of the long piece, line up the board with the marks on the fence and set your stops with a clamp.

When making a stopped cut, hold the work tight to the stop and fence then move down onto the bit. Just move the work along as you rout so you don't burn your way to depth instead of cutting to it. It may take several passes to get to the finished depth, but once you do, make the cut until you reach the far stop. Make the through-cuts next on the shorter end boards. Then raise the bit height to the final depth, finish up the through-cuts, then do the stopped ones. Clean up the round ends of the stopped cuts with your chisel.

LINING THE BOTTOM

I use decorative papers often on the inside of my boxes as a pleasant surprise and contrast to the wood. At a good art store you'll find hundreds of options available and they're usually inexpensive. The adhesive I used to use to lay them down with was a binder called matte medium. It was not cheap. One day a friend of mine walked into my shop and watched me gluing down some paper. He noticed that the smell of the expensive matte medium smelled curiously like the smell of inexpensive water-based polyurethane. Oh, happy discovery—the poly works great as a paper glue.

Cut your plywood exactly to size and your paper oversize by an inch or so. Coat the plywood surface with the water-based poly, then coat the underside of the paper. Lay the paper onto the plywood, stretching it out as you go to eliminate bubbles. Press it flat from the center out to the edges. Then coat the top of the paper with the poly as well. Let the piece dry overnight and trim the excess paper with a knife. Once it's dry, check the fit of the bottom into your grooves, being careful not to peel up the paper at the edges (you can also wrap the paper around the edges if you cut the corners carefully). Then prepare your clamps, dry-fit the box together, and glue up.

BREADBOARD ENDS FOR A TOP

A thin ½" top like this will cup over time without the proper restraint. (Who doesn't need proper restraint from time to time?) A panel floating in a frame is one tried-and-true method of accomplishing this, but using a flat panel with breadboard ends also works. These breadboard ends fit over the ends of your large panel using loose-tenon construction and a little bit of glue at the center of the panel—but the key to success is the spring joint that you add to them.

Take the time to grain-match the boards. With quartersawn ash, matching boards isn't too hard. Hold one board on edge up to another to check their compatibility before committing to cutting your boards to length. Plane a light spring joint on the edges of these boards before gluing them up. This will lock them in place as you glue. Lay your boards together, then fold them apart and place them in the vise. Take a few strokes with your smoothing plane until the edges are good and straight.

Before planing, take the time to tune your handplane on some scrap. Make sure it's cutting smoothly, lightly, and evenly (a good rule for all of my cuts). Coming in on a diagonal, take a few passes over the center of your boards. Just a little gap is all that's required to give you good pressure at the ends.

Glue up your stock, let it dry overnight, then flatten the new board and square its edges and ends. Plane the end grain so it's dead flat before beginning your joinery.

Establish the cut. Use your chisel to establish your cuts and help guide the bandsaw blade.

Stop(s). Establish the beginning and end of the stopped grooves for the box bottom, then clamp stop blocks to your router fence.

There are several methods for cutting the joint in the top and breadboard ends. The loose-tenon method works for a lid this size. It's simple to set up for stopped cuts in all the boards at the router table. Cut the pieces to length and clean up the end grain. Mark the length for the groove and set your stops. Lower each board carefully onto the bit and make your cuts to depth. Then prep loose-tenon stock. I used the offcuts from resawing my stock to thickness and passed one board through the planer to bring it close to thickness. Cut pieces to length, then plane to fit. When the panel fits snug in the breadboard ends, it's time for the final touch.

Cutting a spring joint into the ends keeps them in tight to the panel. Come in at a diagonal to the edge and take two or three handplane passes. Check the fit again and you should now see a small gap in the middle of the panel. Center one clamp to it and see if you can't pull it in good and tight. If you can, you're ready to glue up.

With a top this thin, use some shims to move the boards up higher in your clamps. This will help to prevent any twisting when applying clamping pressure. Put glue only on the center 3" to 4" of the grooves in the breadboard ends, and a dollop in the matching location on the panel (this is where the loose tenons will be inserted). No glue should be applied past this center section because you still have to allow for movement over time. With the spring joint and the loose tenon, you'll get plenty of pressure and support at the edges of the panel. Clean up the panel and breadboard ends, and chamfer the ends on them to match the finger joints.

FINISHING TOUCHES

Finger joints don't need pinning for strength, but if you like the look, add-

Dead flat. Before you start the joinery for the breadboard ends, plane the top's end grain so the end is dead straight.

Loose tenons. Cut your loose tenons to length, then plane them in thickness to fit the groove you cut at the router. Remember that the grain direction of the tenons should run the same as the panel.

Raise your glue-up. With thin stock, it's best to hold the assembly up so that the workpiece is centered in your clamps' jaws. If you skip this step, the clamping pressure could more easily twist the panel.

Template. Mark out the handle shape onto your blank. A template made of MDF or masonite allows for quick transfer of the shape.

Cleanup. Clean up the first bandsaw cut on the handle with a spokeshave or rasp. Work downhill into the hollow to avoid tear out.

ing round pins here is a nice detail. Make up pin stock at the bandsaw, cutting just over the final diameter you want. Plane to size, then chamfer the edges with a block plane before hammering the stock through a dowel plate to size it accurately. Mark out and drill your finger joints, then glue in your pins. A contrasting wood here adds a nice touch.

After hinging the lid with simple butt hinges, add dividers to the inside. I stopped cutting dados for dividers in my box sides when I realized that a tight-fitting length worked just as well. Mill the divider stock to ¼" thickness and trim it exactly to length first. Use a plane and a shooting board to nail the fit. Put the dividers together with half-joints after you decide how you want to divide the inside compartments. Mark their positions and gauge in a line for the depth of cut. You can cut the half-joints at the bandsaw or by hand.

Designing handles is a job I postpone until I can look at the final piece. I first design on paper to find a shape that suits the intention of the box. Then I make up a template to guarantee that I'll get a shape that I like. Templates are quick to make in masonite or MDF and not so precious I can't throw one away. The other reason for using a solid material is that when I have a shape that I really like, I have the template for another handle.

Then I make up several options out of poplar until I find one that works. For purposes of visualizing, a black marker turns the poplar into ebony or walnut; blue and red make it rosewood. My final handle for this box is of walnut cut out on the bandsaw, then shaped and sanded to round the top edges. Cut the handle's top edge first. That way there's still some wood remaining and it's easier to clamp it into the vise to clean up with your spokeshave or rasp. If you need to work out to the end of the handle, clamp one end of it into the vise

Plane to fit. Fit the base boards together using a bench plane with a bench hook or shooting board. Plane the long-grain edges of the short boards until they just fit into their notches.

and clamp a stick onto your bench. The handle then rotates into that stick and won't budge as you shape it.

I drilled two pin holes for small dowels into the bottom of the handle, then glued and pinned to the lid.

The base pieces make the jewelry box appear to be floating. I notch the long boards ⅛" deep to capture the shorter ones. Mark out the starting line 4½" in from their ends with a marking gauge. You can cut out the notches on the table saw with a crosscut sled set up with stops, or saw them by hand and use a shoulder plane to get them to depth.

I never try to make the width of the cut perfect. There are too many ways I can find to screw that up!

I cut the notch just a hair undersized in width, then plane the sticks to fit together. I use my bench hook as a shooting board with a No. 4 plane and take just enough passes to get a snug fit. Mark out the short pieces with a gauge line 2½" in from their ends. This is where they'll fit into the longer ones. Check the fit on all the pieces before gluing them up. Use just a spot of glue and clamp the pieces together. You can also run a short dowel pin through the joint to lock them in place.

Finish the inside of any box with shellac—not an oil finish. Oil finish will leave a smell inside that will last, regrettably, forever, and it's not a pleasant smell. Get over your fear of shellac (if you have any) and give it a try. Thin the stuff in the can down with alcohol (or dissolve shellac flakes at a #2-pound cut) so it's easy to apply and add as many light coats as you want.

For a jewelry box like this, add a few drops of a pleasant essential oil, such as jasmine, rose, or vanilla to the shellac. This is guaranteed to make the recipient of this jewelry box barely notice how late it arrives—while you will have the satisfaction of building something that uses just a few great tools.

EXPLODED VIEW

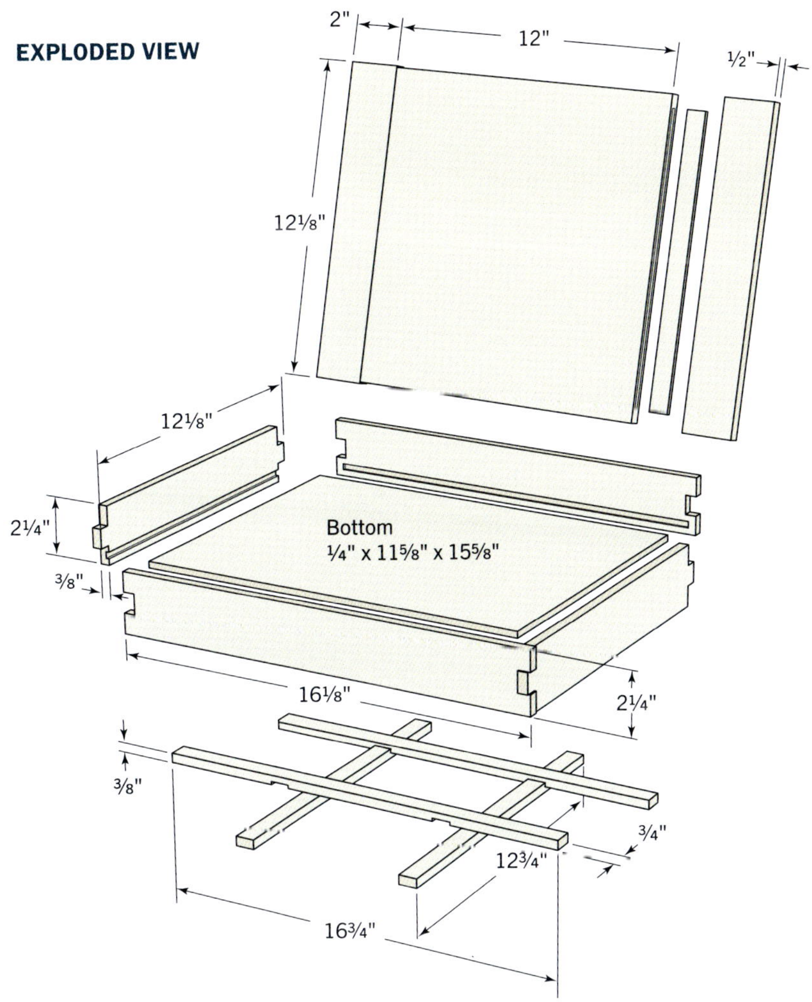

CUT LIST & MATERIALS

	NO.	ITEM	DIMENSIONS (INCHES) T	W	L	MATERIAL
☐	2	Front/back	⅜	2¼	16⅛	Ash
☐	2	Sides	⅜	2¼	12⅛	Ash
☐	1	Top	½	12	12	Ash
☐	2	Breadboard ends	½	2	12⅛	Ash
☐	2	Front baseboards	⅜	¾	16⅞	Ash
☐	2	Side baseboards	⅜	¾	12⅞	Ash
☐	1	Bottom	¼	11⅝	15⅝	Plywood
☐	2	Butt hinges				
☐	2	Long base pieces	⅜	¾	16¾	Ash
☐	2	Short base pieces	⅜	¾	12¾	Ash
☐	*	Dividers	¼	*	*	*Cut to fit; design as desired
☐	1	Handle	½	1	11	Contrasting wood

INLAID (BIBLE?) BOX

Scholars question whether these boxes actually held the family's Bible; regardless, this Pennsylvania-designed box deserves high praise.

BY GLEN D. HUEY

From the minute I brought this lidded box into the *Popular Woodworking* office, debate began. I called it a Bible box, but some wondered where that term originated. Is it a name coined by those looking to build an interest in these boxes so they could sell them for a profit? Or is that term what the original owner used in 1730?

You can call it a Bible box, a lidded box, or whatever you like. I'm going to call it a great project that is an introduction to, or a chance to practice and improve upon, many woodworking techniques, from lathe work to shop-made herringbone inlay to half-blind dovetails. And it's a project that I've had on my "to build" list for many years.

Thin, but not too thin. With ⅝" material, you'll want to leave an area beyond the dovetails that's thick, but anything extra is pulled from the dovetails and that causes tedious work at the joints.

Go past the line. Over-cut lines are found on many, if not most, of the antique pieces we hold in the highest esteem. The extra sawing pays dividends as you remove the waste material to form the pins.

Tweak the corners. Work carefully as you remove the waste to create the pins. If the edge becomes damaged, it shows forever.

Pinpoint accuracy. Lip the marking gauge cutter just past the end of the tail socket to ensure the tails are the correct length.

FOUR DOVETAILED CORNERS

This box is assembled with half-blind dovetails at both the front and rear. Half-blind dovetails are required on the front, because you need an un-interrupted surface for the inlay. You could join the rear corners of the box with through-dovetails as was done on the original, but I chose to keep the joinery the same at both front and back so I could choose the best-looking joints for the front of my box after it was assembled.

Whether it's pins first or tails first for you, the pin boards should be the front and rear box pieces. Cut your tails in the end pieces. I set the marking gauge to leave ⅛" thickness between the pins and the face of the boards.

Perfectly matched. Make sure your tail board is matched to the pin board as you transfer the layout. Any variations affect your joint fit.

LEAD PHOTO BY AL PARRISH; STEP PHOTOS BY THE AUTHOR; ILLUSTRATIONS BY ROBERT W. LANG

Wrenched to size. Feet tenons need to fit tight, so an easy measurement setter is an open-ended wrench. Work slowly; as the wrench slides over the tenon, the tenon is the right size.

As I worked on the dovetails, I had no troubles. Later, however, as the grooves were cut for the inlay, I found that this thin area was rather delicate and weak. So, when I build another box, I'll mark the thickness at around 3⁄16" (if you leave it too thick, the tails begin to lose their holding power, especially if you're using a 1:6 dovetail ratio—I use a 12° dovetail angle).

If you're new to dovetails, there's tons of information available, scads of articles written, and more than a few videos that will walk you through the dovetail process. So as not to be redundant (and for brevity), I'll relate just a couple dovetail pointers that I find helpful.

First, do the layout work on your box pieces. To this day, I saw lines that are drawn on the workpieces and extend the saw cuts beyond the baseline on the face of the pin board—hold to the lines on the pin board ends.

Second, as you begin to remove that waste, take small cuts at the corners of the dovetail area and work slowly. As your chisel displaces the waste, it drives the material upward against the pin—any damage is there forever. If you work slowly and in small steps, the chisel drives the waste upward and along the beveled edge of the pin; this process keeps the pins intact. Work both corners of the waste, then remove the center portion as you progress to the scribe line.

Another tip for half-blind dovetails deals with how you set your marking gauge when establishing the baseline for your tails. It's best to set the gauge wheel or cutter just past the previously scribed baseline of the pin board (p. 15, middle right). This ensures the resulting tails are the exact length needed to fill the area without any small gaps in the fit.

Marked for boring. A marking gauge easily sets the location for the feet tenons. Mark from each corner to find the hole's center.

Tight fit becomes tighter. The fit of the foot tenons to their holes should be snug, but add a wedge in each saw cut and the fit is locked in place. Cut the wedge flush after installation.

FOOT & MOLDING DETAILS

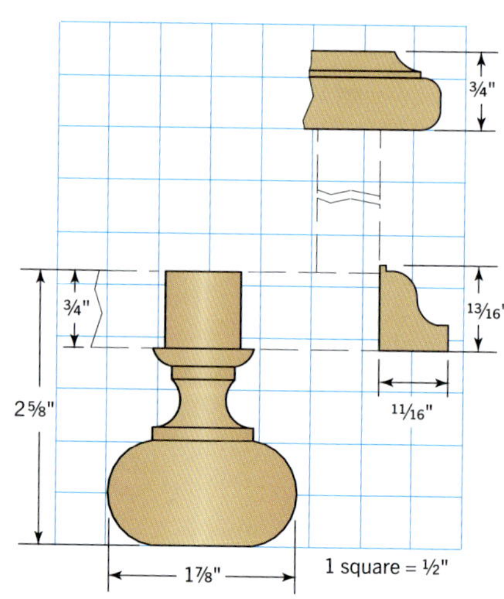

Scribe your box end pieces on both faces, then position the pin board to transfer the layout to your tail board. It's helpful to find a way to hold the pin board vertical so you can slip the tail board into position (just at the scribe line) while you keep your hands free from a balancing act as the layout is transferred.

Complete and test-fit your joints, but don't glue up any of the corners yet. There is still work to do to prepare for the herringbone inlay.

BOTTOMS UP

With final dimensions available from the completed box, we can size the box bottom and turn and install the ball feet.

The ball feet in this project are a great introduction to turning. The sizes are small, but the turning is detailed. Chuck your stock into the lathe and turn four feet to profile, keeping these thoughts in mind as you turn: The four feet are positioned at the corners of the box, set away from each other. In fact, each foot is located away from the corner, as well, presenting a shadowy overhang that covers a portion of the foot. Also, the feet are 1⅞" tall, so it's all-but-impossible to see more than two of the feet at any one time as the box sits.

What I'm driving at is that you should turn the feet as close to the provided profile as you can, but please don't get caught up in the idea that each foot should be perfect. Don't get bogged down in the process and become discouraged. The feet aren't the focus of the piece. Just get them turned as nicely as you can then move on.

That said, there is one part of the turning that should be accurate—the tenon that's used to attach the feet to the box bottom. The tenons need to be properly sized so you can drill a hole (¾"), slide the feet into the bottom, and

EXPLODED VIEW

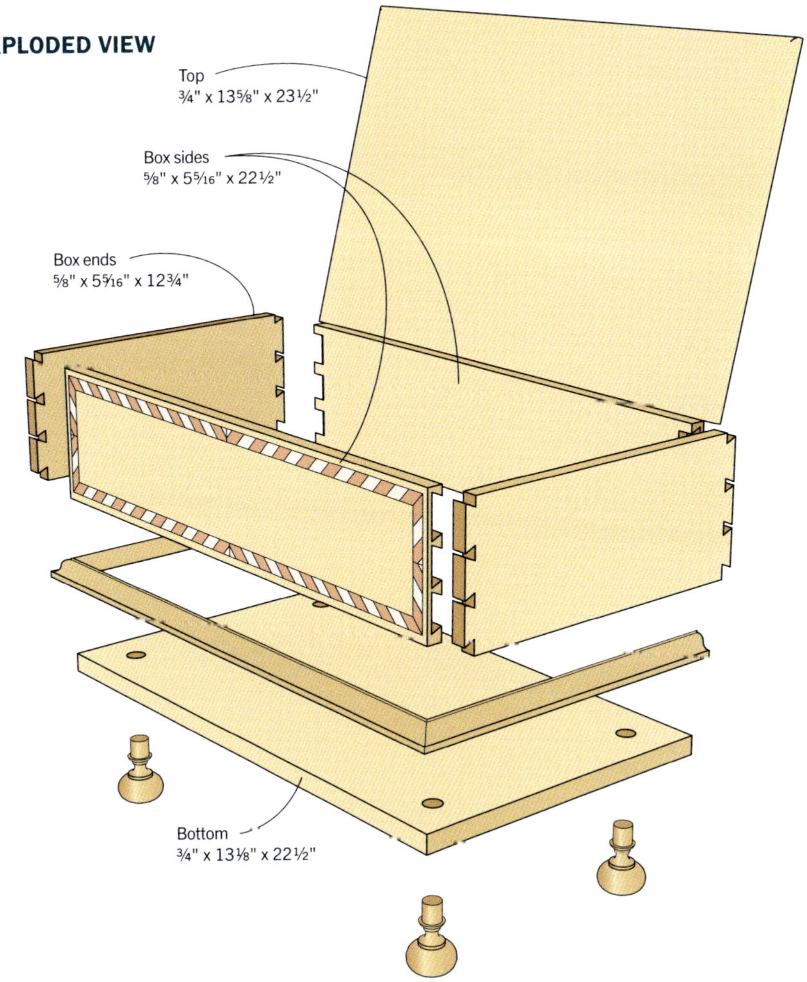

CUT LIST & MATERIALS

	NO.	ITEM	DIMENSIONS (INCHES) T	W	L	MATERIAL	COMMENTS
☐	2	Box sides	⅝	5⁵⁄₁₆	22½	Walnut	
☐	2	Box ends	⅝	5⁵⁄₁₆	12¾	Walnut	
☐	1	Bottom	¾	13⅛	22½	Walnut	
☐	4	Feet	1⅞	1⅞	2⅝	Walnut	
☐	1	Top	¾	13⅝	23½	Walnut	
☐	10	#1 Inlay	¾	⁷⁄₁₆	12	Cherry	
☐	10	#2 Inlay	¾	⁷⁄₁₆	12	Maple	
☐	1	Stringing	¾	3	12	Maple	¹⁄₁₆" strips
☐	4	Wedges	¾	⅛	⅝	Oak	Cut from wide piece
☐	2	Fixed-pin hinges		1½	2		
☐	1	Lock				Antique brass	
☐	1	Escutcheon				Antique brass	

have a snug fit. A trick I like when sizing turnings to a specific measurement is to use an open-ended wrench as a gauge. Turn the tenon area to an approximate size, then continually check the size with a wrench that matches the specific measurement you're after.

Mill your box bottom to size (based on your joined box) and to thickness. This is a place to use lesser-quality lumber. My box bottom contains several areas of sapwood that I would never use in a "show" position.

Set your marking gauge to 1¾", then find the location for each of the four feet (p. 16, bottom left). After the lines are set, the holes need to be bored completely through the bottom. If a drill press is your tool of choice, there are no worries. But if you're into hand tools and plan to use a brace and bit, make sure the hole is bored at 90° to the face. The foot has to fit square to the bottom to keep the look right.

Slide each foot tenon into its hole, then cut the length of the tenons to match the thickness of the bottom. Each tenon is wedged after it is installed through the box bottom. (I made the wedges from a scrap of oak I had in the shop, but any wood does the job.) Make a single cut across the grain of the foot for the wedge. Placing the cut across the growth rings allows the tenon to expand and tighten to the hole as the wedge is inserted without the possibility that the foot could split as the wedge is driven—as might be the case if the cut was parallel to the growth rings.

Slide the tenon into the hole, ensuring that the foot is tight to the underside of the bottom; add a small amount of glue on the wedge, then drive the piece into the tenon. Complete the installation of all four feet, trim the extra length from each wedge, then set the assembly aside.

Define the cut. It's important to establish the router bit's start and stop cut lines to accurately create the inlay grooves. Rotate the bit to determine the edge of the cut, then mark both locations on an auxiliary fence that's locked in position.

Plunge cut at the start. Layout lines on the rear of the box front are matched to the layout lines on the fence in order to accurately cut the inlay groove. The start of the cut is shown here.

Move with slow & steady hands. As the trailing line aligns with the second fence line, the groove is complete. It's better to stay short of the lines and finish the groove with a chisel.

Scraps of design. There's nothing more satisfying than to use shop scraps. Here you see the beginning of the shop-made inlay. Positioning the pieces at a 45° angle as assembled increases the yield of inlay.

Not a random rip. Sizing the pieces of assembled scraps is important to the overall task. All the parts of the inlay add up to match the width of your groove.

Thin is in. String pieces border the herringbone strips. Set your fence to leave the string pieces as cutoffs—that's the safest method to produce multiple thin pieces.

It's good to be strong. Inlay pieces assembled with glue and clamped with rubber bands are slightly wider than the groove size.

INLAY PREPARATION

The grooves for the inlay are cut at a router table with a drop-cut action. The process is not difficult, but does require accuracy in setup. You may wish to make the grooves with a plunge router—if you're more comfortable using that tool, go for it.

Step one is to position the router table fence after a bit is installed. The groove is ½" wide and 3⁄32" deep; any straight ½"-diameter router bit works. Position the fence with ¼" between the blade and the fence. Use a scrap to test and adjust the fence setting; the final position is important.

Next, mark lines on your fence to indicate the exact cut of the router bit—one mark on each side of the bit. To find the lines, slide a square end of an offcut to just touch the router bit cutting edge (with the tool unplugged, of course). Rotate the bit until the cut-off stops being pushed away from the bit. Mark that location on your fence. Repeat the same process on the other side of the bit to complete the marking.

There is some layout work on the front piece to establish the start and stop lines of the router cut. With the distance between the fence and the router bit set at ¼" (that leaves ¼" of box front before the inlay begins), you need to match that distance with the start and stop lines. Pull in ¼" from each corner and make a pencil line on the backside of the box front.

The idea is to drop-cut the workpiece onto the router bit with the start line aligned with the proper line on the router table fence. Continue through the cut until the stop line aligns with the opposite fence line, then remove the workpiece from the cut.

I've found that it's best to stay shy of the fence lines whether you are at the start or the stop end of the cut. That way you won't cut away too much wood, and you can clean up and straighten the grooves with your chisels. You'll need to square each corner by hand anyway.

The grooves for the long sides of the box front are easy to rout. It's the short ends that are a bit trickier—it's harder to keep the box front square and tight to the router fence as you work. Work these two cuts with care. After the grooves are complete, straighten any lines and square the corners.

SHOP-MADE HERRINGBONE

Most of us have scrap piled high in our shops. The inlay used on the front of this box puts some of that scrap to work. The process is simple. You add a personal touch to the box, and you'll save money because you don't have to purchase the inlay.

For starters, select a couple woods that complement your box. I like cherry and maple for inlay into a walnut box, but the original piece only had white cedar as the inlay. Whether you use hardwood or softwood, the creative steps are the same.

Begin with 10 strips of each color that are ¾" thick and 7⁄16" wide; wider strips begin to look too bulky in the completed inlay. Alternate the species then assemble the pieces into a plank. To save material (even scraps are valuable!), glue the pieces at or near a 45° angle (p. 18, middle right).

After the glue-up dries, flatten both faces parallel to one another, keeping the panel as thick as possible. Cut the assembly at 45° to create an edge to take small rips off. Next, slice the ⅜"-thick pieces from the panel. Why ⅜"? You need to work the inlay to fit into the ½" groove cut in the box front, so with the herringbone at ⅜" you can add a 1⁄16" piece of string to both sides to arrive at the ½" size.

To make the 1⁄16" stringing pieces, rip pieces from wide stock at your table saw. Mill and square a piece of stock then just cut the stock at the table saw so as to clean up the second edge—note

The last step. Strips of herringbone inlay are ripped at a bandsaw to produce the final pieces. Plane the faces before work at the bandsaw commences and keep the pieces thicker than the groove is deep.

Check the fit. The key to fitting the inlay is to use sandpaper to work the edges so the fit is tight and to begin at the corners to establish the color matches.

the fence setting. Next, slide the fence toward the blade enough to compensate for the blade thickness and provide a 1⁄16" strip—stay on the thick side more than thin. It's better to have the assembled strip a wee bit stronger than ½". Repeat the steps to produce the second string strip.

Now it's time to assemble the pieces. Add glue to both faces of the herringbone pieces, position a 1⁄16" strip on each side, and add clamps. For this type of work, my favorite clamps are ordinary rubber bands. Twist the bands around the glue-up a number of times until tight, then slide the band along the inlay so there are no small gaps when complete.

After the glue is dry, clean up the faces with your handplane; then, using a bandsaw, cut pieces that are slightly thicker than the grooves are deep (3⁄32"). Clean up the face after each cut. You'll need five or six pieces of finished inlay to complete the box front. Each group should yield three or four pieces, so assemble at least two.

INLAY INSTALLATION

With the pieces of inlay in hand, you'll need to fit the pieces into the grooves of the box front. This step is pretty self-explanatory, but here are a couple hints to smooth out any small bumps.

With the inlay matched closely to the groove width, there should be little work to do on the pieces to get them to fit. A piece of 120-grit sandpaper adjusts the inlay where needed on the edges. Work carefully and check the fit as you progress.

As the pieces are fit, the corners need to be trimmed. A square end of a block is a big help to get the cuts just right. Mark where you wish to cut the inlay, position the block, add a bit of downward pressure on the block to hold everything in place, then make the cut keeping your saw tight against the block. The worst that could happen is you tilt away from the block as you make the cut, and that would cause the inlay to have the slightest bevel. That's great when fitting two pieces of inlay together, but don't overdo it. This allows the top edges of the inlay to meet for tight seams.

A block works great when you need to trim the inlay with a chisel as well. Take a close look at the photos of the box. The inlay reverses at the middle of each run. This was common practice when the box was built. Fit the inlay to the corner first. Find the center point of the run, then trim the piece with a square cut. If you match opposing hardwoods at the corners, the center meeting point should show mirrored images.

After the inlay is fit to the box, remove the pieces, apply glue to the grooves and to the back face of the inlay, then place the strips back in position. Add a piece of waxed paper over the inlay to stop potential glue transfer, position another similar-sized piece on top, then apply a few clamps to hold everything while the glue dries.

As the front comes out of the clamps, it's a great time to prep for the installation of the lock and the escutcheon. Of course, you can do that after the box is assembled, but the area is more confined and the work requires a bit more patience.

WRAP UP CONSTRUCTION

So far, all the work has been on individual pieces. It's time now to assemble the box. Add glue to the dovetail joints (remember those?) and slip the joints together. Use a square to check the box, or measure the diagonals, then set the box aside.

As the box dries, mill the material for the top according to the cut list. Use your favorite router bit profile on the ends and front edge. I used a cove and bead bit on the top edge and a small roundover bit on the bottom edge to complete the profile.

After the glue has dried, attach the bottom and feet to the box. Nails are the answer for this job because the nails allow for some seasonal movement. Drill pilot holes then drive the finish nails through the bottom into the box. Set the nails just below the surface.

Sand the assembled box through 180 grit, making sure to level the inlay and to true up the bottom edges to the box on all four sides.

After the sanding is complete, it's time to make and install your bottom moldings. Profile the edges of a wider piece of stock with a small-diameter Roman ogee router bit, then rip the molding off that stock. The molding wraps three sides of the box and is

It's a quick trim. With the inlay design at 45°, the fit at the corners is easy. Use a square block end to guide your saw as you make the initial cut.

Fine-tune for looks. That same square block end acts as a guide for your chisel when fine-tuning the fit of the corners. If you undercut the end just a bit, the fit at the top of the inlay is sure to be tight.

There's a method to the madness. The inlay is not randomly added to the front. Notice each corner has two opposing colors matched and that each run is split at the center with the half-runs being mirrored images.

Nail, don't glue. The bottom of the box is attached with nails. The nails hold tight, but allow for seasonal movements in the cross-grain application.

The finish is as easy as the box. There's no need for stain or dyes that would color the inlay. Boiled linseed oil (one coat) and shellac makes the walnut sing and the inlay stand at attention.

attached with glue and brads. Notice that the molding is taller than the thickness of the box bottom. The extra 1⁄16" makes sure the joint between the box and bottom is hidden.

The top is a snap. Mill the top according to the cut list—or size it to your box so that there is a ½" of overhang on the front and ends. Next, profile those same three edges. I used a cove-and-bead bit on the top edge of the piece and a 3⁄16" roundover bit to shape the bottom edge, leaving a bullnose profile behind.

After the work is complete and the top is sanded, mount the hinges that join the top to the box. I like to waste away as much of the area as possible, then finish the work with hand tools. Set the hinges to the top first, then position the top to the box and transfer the hinge location. Fit the lid tight to the box, but without any binding.

FINISHING THE BOX

Stain or dye is not a wise choice, in my opinion. These would color the inlay and that's not a good thing. A natural finish is best. I chose shellac as a topcoat after a single coat of boiled linseed oil. A few coats, either brushed, ragged, or sprayed on, and you're done. Sand the surface between coats to keep things smooth and use 0000 steel wool to knock the high sheen off the box when the application is complete. There is no finish on the inside of the box.

This box is a great place to store the family Bible—but if you're not a member of the "Bible box" crowd, it's still a fun piece to build and an excellent test of one's woodworking skills.

Built with love. The wild apple top was the starting point for this "memories box" I made for my wife. The rest of the box is made of Swiss pear.

KRENOV-STYLE MEMORIES BOX

Wood is the starting point of inspiration for these boxes infused with the past.

BY TED BROWN

In my mind, this article goes to the root of why we work wood. It is about the philosophy of creating things in wood and the approach, more so than the technical application of skill. Back in 1993, I spent nine months studying a way of working under James Krenov at the College of the Redwoods in Fort Bragg, Calif. Yes, I learned technical things there, but more important is that Jim inspired us to think, to be sensitive in our choices, and to do the very best we could in the execution.

If you have read Jim's books, you will immediately grasp the fact that his way of working was significantly different from the rest. Jim was excited by the wood itself, and how he could gently massage the material to create a piece with a natural look, with a feeling. I once heard him say something along the lines of, "When you look at a piece of fine furniture, you are not just looking at the piece, but a significant portion of the maker's life."

Surprise. Inside the larger box is the surprise of a smaller one.

Scene. For the top panel of your box, choose wood that creates an inviting visual scene.

Does it look right? Don't be beholden to measurements. If the visual weight of the frame looks right, then it is right.

This article is about applying and enjoying the principles I learned from Jim. It is about the making of three small boxes: why they were made, for whom they were made, and what considerations went into the materials, shapes, weights, and feel of each piece. Jim liked fine work, a good honest joint, thoughtful use of grain, and little tool marks left by the maker in the wood.

I made these boxes for people I love. The first, made of Swiss pear, was built for my parents. It is a "memories box"—not that different from a jewelry box, except that there are fewer little pockets inside. The idea is to store bits of your life in these boxes: photos, ticket stubs, documents, awards, trinkets—just about anything that sparks your memory of special people and special times. The second box, also in Swiss pear, was made for my girlfriend, now my wife. In the same way that I selected a favorite feminine wood for my mother, I also selected Swiss pear for my dear wife. The third box I made was of curly maple and ziricote.

FREE YOURSELF IN YOUR WORK

Jim taught us to focus on the visuals in the wood. In this case, when making a box, the most important visual is the top, or "face," of the piece. This becomes the starting point—finding a piece of wood with an interesting message for the top panel of the box. If the panel is interesting, then the piece becomes alive and inviting. If the carcase of the box is smooth and calling out for your touch, then you move to a second level of tactile enjoyment.

In the case of the box made for my wife, the idea started with an interesting piece of wild apple wood. I knew that the graphics were strong, that the fine fruitwood would work well with my plane, and that the tight grain would take an exquisite finish. The panel looks like a country scene, with a horizon, and a setting sun in the west. Surrounding that image with a frame of Swiss pear made for an interesting beginning to a lovely box. When you open the box, you use an integrally carved handle, yet another Krenov influence, keeping a natural relationship to the piece.

Yet another influence was the creation of a little surprise inside. When you open the box, you find another delicate box. This box is made of curly maple, and it sports the rich hues of caramel and licorice in the Macassar ebony bottom. In the bottom of the larger box, light curly maple is used to effectively give a sense of light from within. The rails on which the inner box is perched are hard maple, waxed so that the little box can slide along with ease. It is all about the little things.

Jim taught us how to create an entire piece without getting caught up in measuring or numbers. Along with that concept, he spoke to the idea of "visual weight." That is, how thick should a frame member be? How wide? How big should the box itself be? It is a very freeing way of working when you allow the process to be driven by discovery. The box should be about "this wide by this long," he would say, waving his hands about. That concept would then get more focused by the size of the pattern of the top panel.

Once the top panel is sized, we then place the frame material around it, and mark the visual weight of the frame width on each piece. The frame members will all be milled at the same time, so the thickness of each is exactly the same, and "about this thick," as Jim would say, as he looked at his thumb and forefinger. The point was this: The thickness of the frame had to be the right visual weight for the size of the box. Jim encouraged us to avoid round numbers such as ½" and ¾", because those numbers handcuff you, and the resulting design looks that way. I actually run the parts (plus one extra) through the planer all at the same time, and stop milling when the thickness looks right.

KEEP YOUR WORK WELL-ORIENTED

Cabinetmaker's marks serve several purposes. We use a system based on a triangle. The bottom of the triangle is placed on the bottom of the frame, the stiles or sides of the frame get the sides of the triangle, and the top frame member gets the tip of the triangle.

This marking scheme allows us to keep the frame members oriented, and—this is very important—with the correct side up, when cutting joinery and grooving the frame to accept the panel.

When laying out the mortise positions, I simply estimate two things: how far I want to stay away from the outside of the frame, and how far I must stay away from the inside of the frame so that the panel groove does not cut into the floating tenon. I take a piece of wood and create a story stick from which I transfer the location of each mortise. Those cabinetmaker's marks save me all the time from making errors: no numbers—simple and sensible!

When cutting the mortises, the first thing I look for are the cabinetmaker's marks. I want to know that I always have the right side up. In this way, it does not matter whether or not the mortise is placed in the center of the wood, so setting the mortising machine

Stay oriented. Cabinetmaker's marks help you instantly see which face is up, and keep your pieces oriented. Mark them on blue tape and you won't mar your planed workpieces.

Floating tenons. A horizontal boring machine cuts the mortises for my floating tenons.

Story stick. Used to probe the depth of the mortise, the story stick is then used to transfer that measurement to the tenon. Cut the tenon a little shorter than the mortise depth.

is just as easy as eyeballing the middle of the frame thickness.

With the mortises cut, I then proceed to install floating tenons into either end of the stiles. I glue the tenons in place, leaving too much material protruding, in terms of length. When I dry-fit the tenons into the rails, it is simply a matter of gauging the depth of the mortise with a small story stick. I mark the depth of the mortise on the story stick, then transfer that depth to the tenon and cut the tenon a little short so that it will not bottom out.

RAISE THE PANEL

The panel is raised. I do this with a modified straight router cutter, which has had its tips rounded slightly to make a wee rounded rabbet in the wood. To cut the panel to a tight fit in the frame, I again use two thin story sticks—material thinner than the groove, cut so that it just fits into the groove for length and width. With the ends of the story sticks cut to a point, you can slowly nibble off the points of the sticks with a chisel, until the stick just fits into the groove with a snug fit.

Use the short stick to set the bandsaw fence to a setting for the panel width, and the longer stick to set up the table saw to cut the panel length. Raise the panel with the router table, then take a few plane strokes off the width of either side of the panel to allow for seasonal movement. I usually eyeball my estimate for movement of the panel, mark that with a finger gauged pencil line, then plane to the line. Still no numbers.

The panel is left just slightly too thick during raising so that, as the panel is handplaned, the thickness is planed on the backside to a nice fit with the groove. While you have the handplane out, it is time to plane the insides of the box sides before dovetailing.

DISTINCTIVE DOVETAILS

Make your dovetail pattern interesting, and something that cannot be replicated by router cutting. Jim always cut his pins first, tuned them with a sharp chisel for shape, and fit the tails to that.

Dovetails are cut to scribelines made with a marking gauge, and set so that the pins and tails will protrude just a bit, just enough to be cleaned up to a perfect finish when the outside of the box is handplaned.

Then, yes, I sand a bit with 400-grit paper. Jim would say to soften the edges until they feel good, but not so much that they feel like a marshmallow. Rounding over the edges starts with a plane and a file, and is then refined with a little bit of fine sandpaper, in that order.

AN INVITING FINISH

This sort of box is all about creating a delicate piece that calls out to be handled. In that vein, Jim taught us to use

MATERIALS*

	NO.	ITEM	COMMENTS
OUTER BOX			
☐	1	Top panel	Choose an interesting piece
☐	4	Top frame pieces	
☐	4	Box sides	
☐	1	Bottom	
☐	2	Interior rails	
☐	2	Hinges	
INTERIOR BOX			
☐	4	Box sides	
☐	1	Bottom	

*Krenov-style boxes are sized to feel right, not constrained to exact measurements.

Pare. Tune your pins with a sharp chisel for the perfect shape before transferring the shape to your tail board.

Distinct dovetails. Lay out an interesting dovetail pattern—one that can't be cut with a router and jig—to instantly signal your box is handmade.

shellac polish to finish the piece. Again, even in the dilution of the flakes in the alcohol, it was "put about that much in the bottom of the jar, and about three to four times that much alcohol, and swirl it."

The shellac is applied using a padding technique, where the "pillow" of

A BOX FOR MY PARENTS

When I returned from California in 1994, I asked Mom what I could make for their home. She thought for a while, and finally said that she didn't know, that their house was full. She was right. At that stage in their lives my folks had all they needed. So I decided to build them a memories box. Now that my folks are gone, I keep their precious things in it to remember them by.

In this image you see a box with a map hanging over the edge. It is printed on silk, and was sewn into the uniform my father wore while he was in World War II, flying in Lancaster bombers as a wireless air gunner for the Royal Canadian Air Force.

There are many things in this box, from my parents' wedding invitation, to rings, to tickets my dad bought for a train in Montreal on the way home from Europe in 1945.

Make a memories box and give it to your loved ones. And Jim, I will carry your lessons with me forever.

Shellac. Build up to eight coats of shellac, cutting back the finish between each coat with 0000 steel wool. The final step is to apply a fine cabinetmaker's wax such as Clapham's, then cut back that finish with 0000 steel wool once again. The steel wool imparts a tiny scratch pattern in the finish to reduce shine. Buff the box with a soft cotton cloth—what we want is a beautiful soft sheen.

clean white cotton is kept moist, but not wet. Lay down layers of shellac, allowing each to dry in between. Drying time increases as the finish builds. Feel the surface with the back of your hand to see if it is dry—a cool surface is still drying. Cut the finish back with 0000 steel wool between coats, and proceed until you have a sheen but not a shine.

Achieve a pleasing sheen by cutting back the final coat of shellac (about eight coats on the outside) to avoid a shiny look. A fine cabinetmaker's wax is the last part of the finish, which protects the shellac and improves the feel of the piece.

NOW, ABOUT THOSE MEMORIES ...

We work wood because we enjoy the opportunity to work with such a beautiful material, and, with a sensitive hand and eye, we create a wonderful piece. As furniture makers, we may now continue to enjoy the work, as we present it to our loved ones.

REDISCOVER A SHAKER CLASSIC

A rim and box in contrasting species make an elegant eye-catcher.

BY JOHN WILSON

LEAD PHOTO BY AL PARRISH; STEP PHOTOS BY THE AUTHOR; ILLUSTRATIONS BY DAN PESSELL FROM THE AUTHOR'S DRAWINGS

Open boxes, as useful as they are attractive, were not made to hold sweets for the table. Instead, they were for something that makes me wince: expectoration of chewing tobacco. These round open boxes with rims were filled with fresh wood shavings for chewing brethren and visitors, to keep the tobacco users from fouling the pristine floors.

That we hardly ever see this form except in picture books attests to the aversion that such a use fosters. My refusal to name it in the historic way is my hope to change this aversion; "round open box" will do quite nicely to describe this graceful and useful box.

I remember seeing this form with its attractive rim at Hancock Shaker Village, in Hancock, Mass., 25 years ago. And we know they were made at the Mt. Lebanon Shaker Village, in New Lebanon, N.Y., by Daniel Crossman.

The pattern of the finger lap and construction are in the oval box tradition, but the rim is different. Added for strength needed on an object intended for floor use, the rim is a pleasing finishing touch on a box without a lid or a handle. The inside end of this rim band is not feathered; rather it is fitted into the edge of the top finger curve. The band can be ended straight and feathered, or have a single narrow finger. The fastenings are brass escutcheon pins snipped and peened on the inside.

Renaming this historic form for new use in the contemporary home is a fitting way to re-introduce this Shaker classic.

THE PROJECT IN FOUR SIZES

The "Proportions" table (at right) provides three examples (Nos. 1, 3, and 4) from the literature based on historic standards, as well as one size (No. 2) to complete a set for those disposed to graduated nestings. Nos. 1, 2, and 3

Finger & rim detail. The rim is the defining feature on a round Shaker box; it's accentuated by brass escutcheon pins and a maple band to contrast with the cherry of the box band. Note how the rim starts in the curve of the top finger and is feathered at the end for a smooth curve.

PROPORTIONS

	NO. 1	NO. 2	NO. 3	NO. 4
Diameter	7"	8¼"	9½"	11"
Band (l, w)	3¼" x 29"	3⅜" x 33"	3½" x 39½"	5¼" x 43"
Band thickness	5⁄64"–3⁄32"	3⁄32"–7⁄64"	7⁄64"–⅛"	7⁄64"–⅛"
Rim	⅜" x 27½"	⅜" x 31"	7⁄16" x 35"	7⁄16" x 40½"
Fingers	3; 2¼" long	3; 2⅜" long	3; 2½" long	4; 2⅝" long
Circumference	22½"	26¼"	30¼"	34¾"
Tack size	#2¼	#2¼	#2¼ or #2½	#2¼ or #2½
Source	Grasselli[1]	Wilson[2]	Myers[3]	Sprigg[4]

Sources:

[1]Steve Grasselli, oval box craftsman, Syracuse, N.Y., from example in Hancock Shaker Village collection.

[2]John Wilson, the Home Shop, Charlotte, Mich., provides an intermediate size in a nesting series.

[3]D. Clifford Myers, "Oval Boxes" in *Simple Gifts, 25 Authentic Shaker Craft Projects*, by the Editors of Garden Way Publishing, Storey Communications 1990.

[4]June Sprigg, description of object #53 (not photographed) in *Shaker Design*, Whitney Museum of American Art 1986, p. 185.

FINGER PATTERNS

NO. 1
7"-diameter

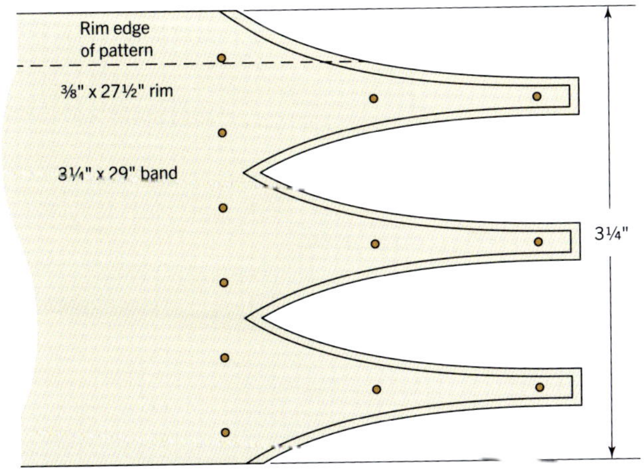

NO. 2
8¼"-diameter

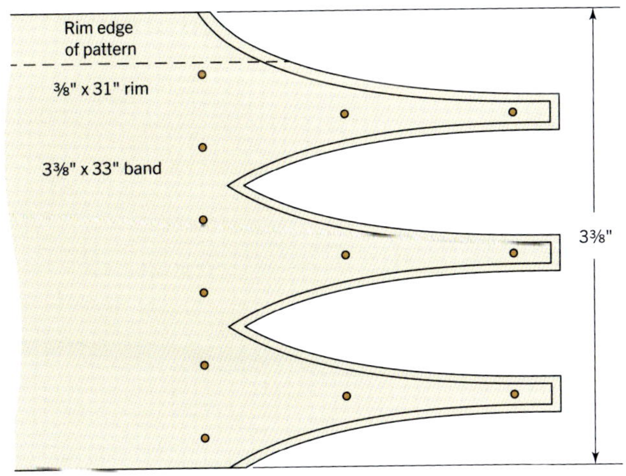

NO. 3
9½"-diameter

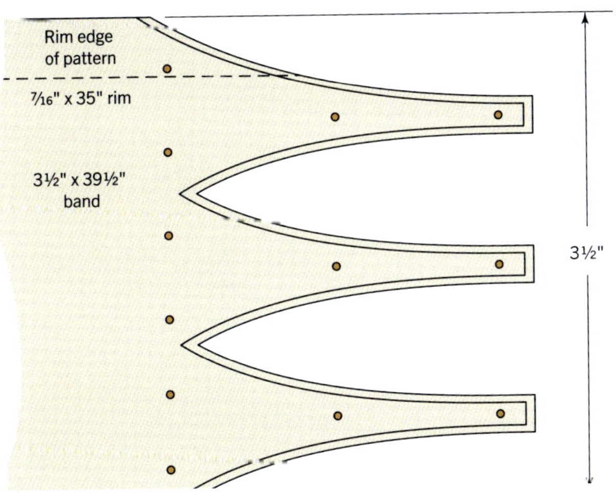

NO. 4
11"-diameter

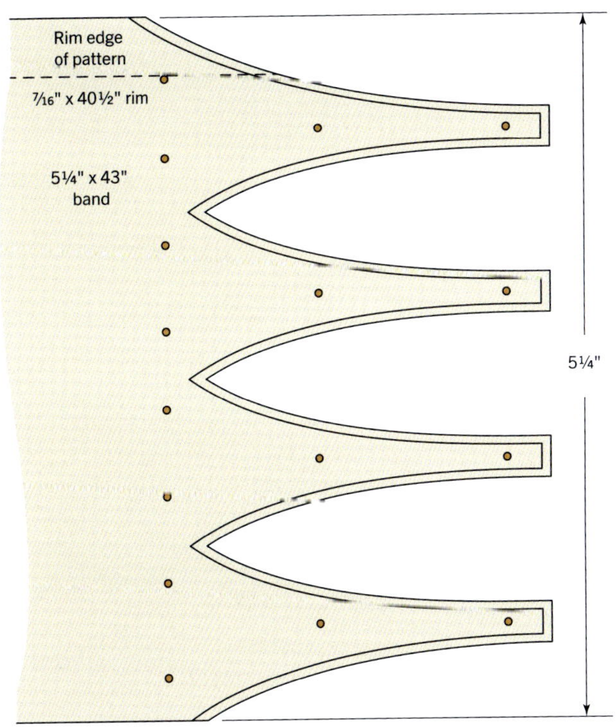

Note that the top finger begins 3/16" farther back than the others. The inside end of the rim will tuck into this space, so be sure not to turn your pattern upside down. (See "Add the Rim" on p. 34.)

Fingers. Use a bandsaw to remove the waste and cut to rough dimensions. Now drill holes in the marked locations for the copper tacks.

Carving. I use a utility knife with a fixed, heavy-duty blade to trim the fingers to final shape, and to cut a slight bevel on the edges.

Feather. Use a belt sander to thin the band stock on the straight end about 2" back to help you more easily bend a fair curve.

will constitute such a set. The largest round, No. 4, has taller sides that fit its proportions.

FINGERS & BANDS

The finger shape and length are similar to those of oval boxes of a similar size with one modification: The top finger begins 3⁄16" farther back (as shown in the drawings on the previous page) to provide the starting point for a rim. Without this, the smaller sizes in particular appear crowded once the rim is in place.

The critical dimension in any bentwood project is the band thickness. The ease of bending, and even the success in completing the project, depends on it. The thinner the wood, the easier and more reliable the bend, but the thicker it is, the stronger the project. In both cases the visual appearance is affected.

The historic range is from 5⁄64" for the 7"-diameter No. 1 box, to 1⁄8" for the 9½"-diameter No. 3 example (see "Proportions"). (Note: An average band thickness of 1⁄10" would work for all four sizes; use #2¼ copper tacks to secure a band of that thickness.)

Box makers understand what a wide range this is, with two different lengths of copper tacks required, depending on thickness.

BENDING & TACKING

Shaker bentwood boxes have the inside end of the band's thickness feathered about 2" so it will blend smoothly. The outside end is cut in distinctive fingers with graceful curved edges that are Gothic in appearance.

After choosing which size box you wish to make, prep your material. Then follow the "Finger Patterns" (p. 31) for the finger shape; trim the cut edges with a knife to create a slight bevel.

Drill 1⁄16" pilot holes for the tacks in the locations marked on the pattern, then thin the finger end about 1" back on a sander to reduce the tips to about half-thickness; that will allow the ends to conform to the curved surface.

Feather the band's inside straight end and outside end back about 2" to almost a knife edge. Shape the rim's inside end to nestle into the band's finger.

Now mark the circumference length on the band. Measure this from the feathered inside end and make a pencil mark near the finger end. After soaking and bending, this marks where the wrapped band will end.

But before you soak the wood, you must prepare a form and shapers for your selected size of round box. The form is simply a 1"-thick foam (or wood) core, cut in a circle the diameter of the box (see "Bending" photo below at right).

Shapers, sometimes called followers or formers, are round wood corks ¾" thick with a 10° beveled edge and two to four 1"-diameter holes for ventilation and finger holds. (See "Snip, file & peen" photo on p. 34.) You'll need two shapers for each box.

You are now ready to soak the band and rim in water to make them pliable. Both water and heat affect the flexibility of the wood. You're probably familiar with how soaking makes wood limber, but heat above 180° F makes lignin soft, which is effective, either alone as in some musical instrument construction, or in combination with soaking. Both hot water and steam-bending are effective for this purpose, with a soaking time of only 10 to 20 minutes. Soaking the pieces in the bathtub also works, but the time is hours, not minutes long (a final rinse with a teakettle of boiling water might help).

CUT LIST & MATERIALS

	NO.	ITEM	DIMENSIONS (INCHES)			MATERIAL
			T	W	L	
☐	1	Sides	See Proportions table			Cherry veneer
☐	1	Bottom	⅜			Quartersawn white pine
☐	1	Rim				Maple veneer
☐		#16 escutcheon pins				Brass
☐		#2¼ tacks				Copper
☐		Toothpicks				

FORMS & CONSTRUCTION

Bending the band around the form will yield an approximate shape. Have the form at the ready as you remove the band from the water. Bend it around the form while hot.

Remove the form and match the feathered end to the pencil-marked circumference line. A scrap wood and spring-clamp arrangement for holding the finger tips will help as you move to the anvil to tack and clinch the fingers.

Now insert the wood shapers at the top and bottom.

RIMS & PINS

With your escutcheon pins at the ready, bend the rim around the top of the band. It begins by neatly tucking into the curve of the top finger. Add a drop of glue under the feathered end before driving the escutcheon pins.

Escutcheon pins have a small half-round head and owe their origin to medieval heraldry objects displayed on a shield (escutcheon) attached with roundhead nails. They are sold in the trim hardware section of stores in various gauge sizes such as the #16, which

In hot water. My copper water tray sits on a hot plate, with wood blocks under each end for stability. A full boil is not necessary; 180° F will soften the lignin sufficiently for bending in about 10–20 minutes.

Bending. Remove the band from the hot water and bend it around the form. You're aiming only for the approximate shape, so don't fuss with wrapping it tightly.

The right size. Remove the form, then match the feathered end to the penciled circumference mark. Use a scrap of wood and spring clamps to hold the fingers in place.

Clinched tacks. Copper tack heads are part of the characteristic look of any Shaker box. Hammer the tacks in place, then clinch the backs on the wet band to make a permanent fastening. If you don't have an anvil, a short length of iron pipe makes an effective surface for driving and clinching. Insert shapers in both sides.

is 1⁄16" diameter, and in various lengths from ½" long. Any length will work, but be sure to buy solid brass rather than brass-plated steel.

The escutcheon pins are among the defining features of this project. The question remains how to work them. They are too thick to clinch and too long to peen. So—after removing the top form—drill 1⁄16" pilot holes every 3" along the rim band, with the final three 2" apart at the feathered end.

Drive pins through the wet band and snip them off inside as close as possible to the wood—closer than diagonal cutters will typically allow. So you'll likely need to file the ends nearly flush after clipping.

Then tap the snipped pins on an anvil or on the inside with a ball peen hammer to slightly peen them.

Reinsert the top form and set the box aside to dry for a few days.

After the box is dry, a drop of glue and spring clamp may be needed to close any gap where the rim begins in the top finger curve.

BOTTOM BOARDS

Traditionally, Shaker box bottom boards were ⅜"-thick quartersawn

Add the rim. The rim gets tucked into the curve of the top finger and ends with a 4" lap that will project about 1" beyond the fingers. After bending the rim in place, remove the top shaper and hold the rim in place (a spring clamp might help) as you drill 1⁄16"-diameter pilot holes every 3" for the escutcheon pins (with three holes 2" apart at the lap).

Snip, file & peen. Snip the end of the escutcheon pins as close as possible, then file them close to flush before peening.

Mark a circle. Once the band and rim are thoroughly dry, the box will hold its round shape, so you can use it as the template for marking the bottom board.

Secure the bottom. I use toothpicks to secure the bottom, drilling 5⁄64" pilot holes every 2"–3" around the box, centered in the thickness of the bottom. After tapping the toothpicks in place, I use side cutters to snip them off, then sand smooth.

white pine (quartersawing minimizes dimensional change with humidity). If you prefer a hardwood bottom, it is better to use a veneered plywood board for dimensional stability to avoid future gaps and breaks. I find that five-ply ¼"-thick birch plywood works well and complements whatever species you select for side bands.

Mark the shape of the round bottom from the dry band itself using a sharp pencil, then cut it at the bandsaw.

Sand up to your lines, giving the edge a 2° bevel angled toward the interior; this will make the bottom wedge into place for a tight fit.

You have a variety of choices to fasten the bottom, from wood pegs (drill 5⁄64"-diameter pilot holes), to copper shoe pegs, to #16 brass escutcheon pins (the latter two both require 1⁄16"-diameter pilot holes).

FINISHING

Round open boxes with rims can be finished similarly to lidded boxes of their day, with milk paint, a colored wash coat, or a clear finish. The choice is yours.

My preference is an oil-based polyurethane varnish because it adds warmth to the wood tone and is durable for the range of uses that the project invites. And, because these boxes have no lids, I finish inside and out. (Finishing the inside of a lidded box traps finish odors, sometimes for years to come. So those I leave unfinished on the interior.)

Use a wipe-on poly or make your own from standard varnish thinned 4:1 with a VMP Naphtha thinner. Keep the project and finish warm (75° F) so thin coats go on easily. Rub the final coat with a brown paper bag to burnish the surface smooth.

This finished project is nothing to spit at. Display it proudly.

Nesting set. Three open boxes (these are Nos. 1, 2 and 3) constitute a set.

JAPANESE SLIDING-LID BOX

This clever and simple piece is great for storing tools, toys, or a kimono.

BY CHRISTOPHER SCHWARZ

While picking though a table of vintage Japanese tools for sale in 2013, I spotted a sliding-lid box under the vendor's table; it was blackened by age, soot, and rust. Despite its scars, however, the box was still graceful and functional.

The owner, a Japanese carpenter, wouldn't part with it. But he let me measure and photograph the piece both inside and out so I could make a respectable version for myself.

The carpenter said it was a toolbox, and it would indeed fit a small kit of tools. But other experts in Japanese furniture said it was more likely a

Make the socket. Hand-cut finger joints are more demanding than dovetails. To ensure you are sawing square and plumb, first make several warm-up kerfs in the waste area before sawing the walls of the socket.

A quick sweep. A coping saw will quickly remove the waste in the socket. Then, chop and pare the remaining waste away with a chisel.

generic storage box that could be used to hold anything—wooden Tupperware, if you will.

The original was made using Douglas fir. I made versions in both vertical-grain fir and Port Orford cedar, another wood preferred by Japanese joiners. The biggest challenge of the project was finding the dome-head nails. I settled on using No. 5, 15 mm dome-head tacks (called "taiko byo") for Japanese drum making, though upholstery tacks with a head ½" diameter or smaller are more economical.

Construction is simple, yet achieving perfection is difficult thanks to all the small details. The corners of the box are joined by finger joints. Everything is reinforced by the dome-head nails.

FINGER JOINTS

The finger joints at the corners of the carcase are quite large. This makes the layout simple, but the execution a challenge. I first laid out and cut the single socket on the side pieces, then transferred that shape to the ends to cut the single pin.

Don't forget that the sockets are ⅝" deep in ½"-thick material. This creates an ⅛" overlap at the box's corners and creates nice shadow lines.

After sawing the socket on the side pieces, remove the waste between with a coping saw and a chisel.

After sawing all the sockets, transfer their shapes to the end pieces to cut the single pin on the end of each end piece. To ensure the baseline of the side pieces is mated perfectly with the ends, tack a wooden ruler to the baseline of each side piece. This makes the transfer process foolproof.

Cutting the single pin on the end pieces is a chisel challenge. Saw and cope the waste. Then use a chisel to level the end grain. A square and a little patience will pay off.

No measuring. No matter how good a sawyer you are, every corner joint will be different. Transfer the shape of each socket onto its mating end piece using a knife.

Flat & square. Work to the baseline with a chisel. Take light cuts and confirm the end grain is flat and square to the faces using a square.

ELEVATION

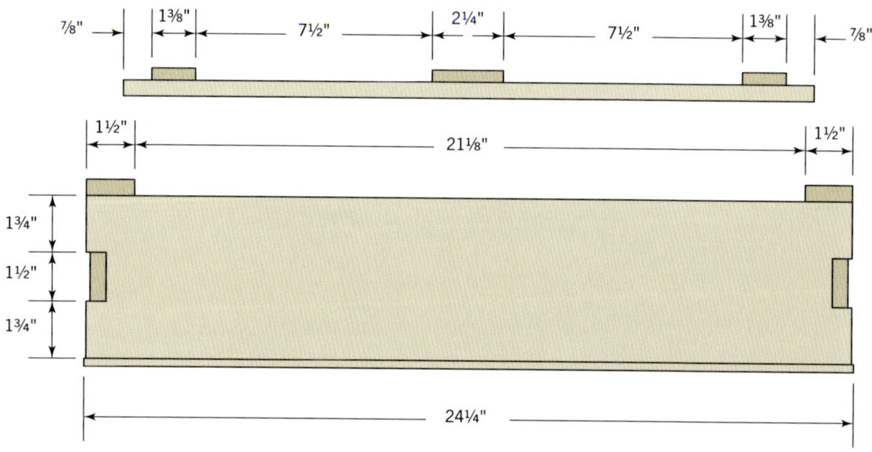

PROFILE

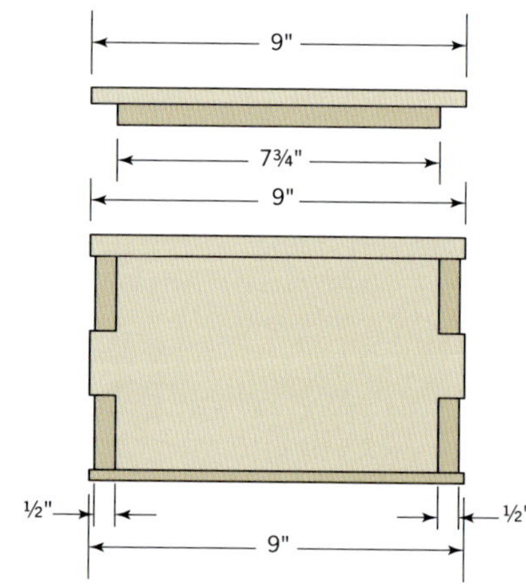

Now fit the joints together. If you have never cut finger joints by hand before, read this next sentence with care: Hand-cut finger joints have to be assembled like dovetail joints.

What does that mean? You can't just hammer the end pieces down into the side pieces. Unless your sawing was perfect—90° in all directions—they won't go together easily, or at all. Instead, slide the end pieces into the side piece sockets to pull up "one way." This might sound confusing until you cut the joint. But it's really no different than realizing that the tailboard and pinboard of a dovetail joint go together in only one way.

The last bit of work before assembly is to chisel a $\frac{1}{16}$" x $\frac{1}{16}$" chamfer on the corners of the finger joints. Lay out the chamfers in pencil, then use a chisel to remove the pencil lines.

ASSEMBLE THE CARCASE

The original box was unfinished—its surfaces were left straight from the plane. Even if you want to apply finish to your box, the overlapping joints at the corners will make cleaning up glue squeeze-out difficult.

So the best thing to do is tape off the joints so glue squeeze-out will end up on the tape. This takes about 10 minutes and makes a world of difference.

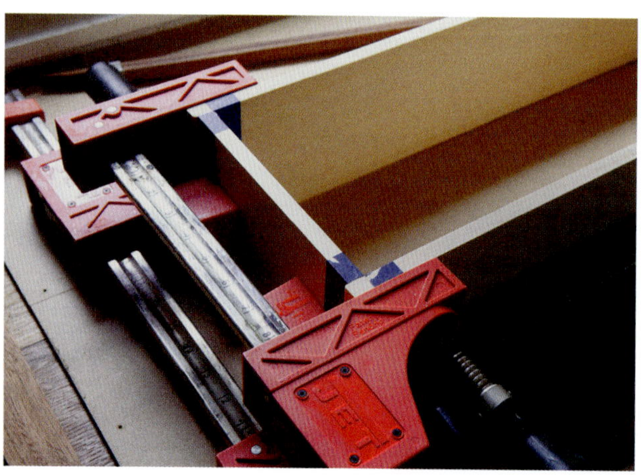

Tape & clamp. Painter's tape protects your planed surfaces from glue. Clamps press the corners tight.

Decorative security. These dome-head nails don't hold as well as a cut nail, but they do add strength and prevent the wood from getting scuffed.

Also, I use liquid hide glue, so clean-up is easy, even if the clamps prevent you from scouring every nook and cranny. After the clamps are off, a little hot water and a toothbrush can remove remaining bits of glue.

After the glue has cured, remove the clamps and the tape, then add the dome-head nails. The drum nails have a thin shank that is square in section. While you could drive these in without a pilot hole, I prefer to bore a 1⁄16"-diameter pilot hole for each nail to prevent its shaft from wandering.

As you can see from the photos below, the nails on the side pieces are not centered; they are "cheated" a bit toward the top and bottom to add holding power to the joint. Drill each pilot hole ½" in from the long end of each side piece. The nails through the end pieces are centered on the pin.

Now add the battens to the case that will capture the lid. These battens are glued and nailed to the ends.

ADD THE BOTTOM

The bottom of the box is thin, nailed on, and overhangs the assembled carcase just a tad. Plane up the bottom piece, then attach it to the carcase with 2d headed nails (1" long). I used cut brads. Again, a 1⁄16" pilot hole is good insurance to prevent the nails from wandering.

The other detail about these brads is that each one is angled a bit—about 7°—to wedge the bottom on the carcase. This is sometimes called "dovetailing" your nails.

After driving the brads in, set the heads 1⁄32" below the surface to prevent

CUT LIST & MATERIALS

	NO.	ITEM	DIMENSIONS (INCHES)			MATERIAL
			T	W	L	
☐	2	Sides	½	5	24⅛	Port Orford cedar
☐	2	Ends	½	5	9	Port Orford cedar
☐	1	Bottom	¼	9	24¼	Port Orford cedar
☐	1	Lid	½	7¾	21¾	Port Orford cedar
☐	2	Small lid battens	½	1⅜	9	Port Orford cedar
☐	1	Large lid batten	½	2¼	9	Port Orford cedar
☐	2	Case battens	½	1½	9	Port Orford cedar
☐		Dome-head nails or tacks	15 mm or ½			Taiko byo, burnished brass, or shiny nickel
☐	2	Tansu handles				Steel

Here's the point. To prevent the battens from sliding around, drive the dome-head nails into each batten so the tips protrude just a bit. Add the glue. Then press the batten in place. The tips of the nails will prevent the batten from sliding.

Look close. The 2d brads are angled just a bit to add some wedging action. This keeps the bottom on through years of service.

the heads from scratching up a nicely finished tabletop.

MAKE THE LID

The lid slides and locks thanks to the battens that are fastened to the lid and the carcase. The dome-head nails alone do not offer enough holding power, so the three lid battens also are screwed to the lid.

I used ⅞" #4 roundhead screws to attach the battens from the inside of the lid. I chose roundhead screws because their heads' shape mimicked the shape of the dome-head nails.

Screw the lid to the battens—two screws per batten—then flip the lid over and add the dome-head nails. Note that the dome-head nails are located a bit more toward the center of the lid than the remainder of the nails on the box. I put them 1½" from the ends of each batten.

Add the pull to one end of the carcase and the box is complete. I left my boxes unfinished, though you could add a coat of wax to the exterior to give it some protection.

While the boxes look nice and crisp now, I look forward to seeing them in 20 years when their scars will make them look even better.

Reinforcements. The screws ensure the battens won't come loose years from now. My stock is perfectly quartersawn, so there isn't much of a concern with wood movement. If your lid will move a lot, you might want to ream out the screws' clearance holes in the lid to allow for movement.

3D VIEW

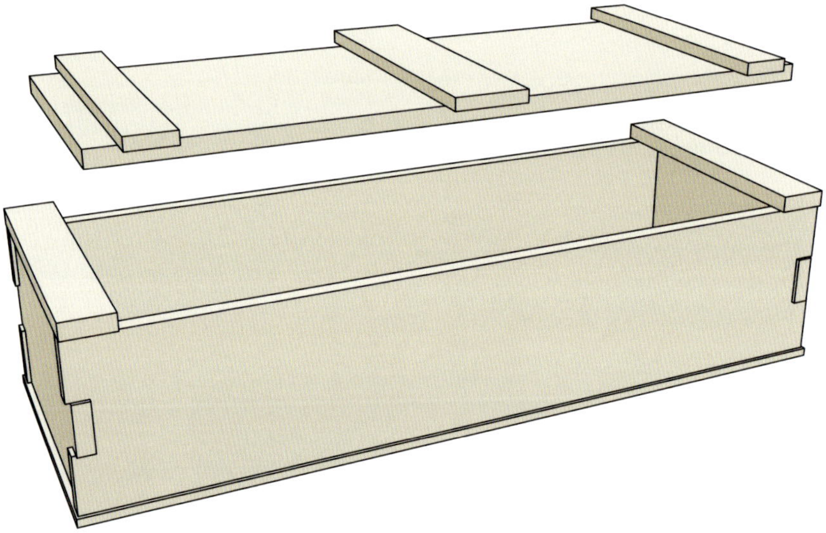

STACKING TOOL CADDY

A simple-to-build tote, perfect for tool and supplies transport.

BY CHAD STANTON

I designed this stacking tool caddy to hold small parts and a few tools. It comprises three tool trays that stack and interlock together to form a single unit that can be carried wherever needed. Best of all, it stores my screws, nails, and small tools so they're all right at hand. It's also handy for transporting other items: sewing supplies, fishing tackle, and whatever else you can think up.

The trays are joined with half-laps secured by dowels. The dowels not only add strength but also add a nice decorative detail to the project. To lock the trays together, the main handle pivots, allowing access to the individual trays. A tongue depressor acts as a simple spring latch.

TRAYS FIRST

The sides for each tray are ½" x 3½" poplar (dimensional ½"x4 lumber from the big box store). To begin the con-

Matching lengths. For clean cuts and a good registration surface, attach an auxiliary fence to the stock fence of the miter saw. Also, ensure consistent lengths by using a stop-block. With the saw off, measure from the blade to the block, and clamp it in place. Start by cutting the end of the board square, then put that end against the stop and make your cuts.

struction, cut the side and end pieces. It's vital they are the same length—if they aren't, the trays won't be square and won't stack and interlock correctly. A stop-block can aid in making the repeat cuts accurately. Cut the short tray sides, then reset the stop-block to cut the long tray sides—you should have six of each.

CUT LIST & MATERIALS

	NO.	ITEM	DIMENSIONS (INCHES)			MATERIAL
			T	W	L	
☐	6	Tray sides	½	3½	19½	Poplar
☐	6	Tray ends	½	3½	8½	Poplar
☐	3	Tray bottoms	½	8½	19	Plywood
☐	2	Handle supports	¾	1½	14¾	Walnut
☐	1	Handle	¾-dia.		21½	Walnut dowel
☐	1	Top tray divider	¾	5½	18½	Walnut
☐	1	Middle tray divider	¾	3	18½	Walnut
☐	2	Handle stops	⅜-dia.		1	Dowel
☐	2	Handle spring latches	⅛	⅝	4*	Tongue depressor
☐	1	Joinery dowel	¼-dia.		**	Walnut
☐	2	Bolts	¼-20		1½	
☐	6	Washers	¼-20			
☐	2	Nuts	¼-20			

*Cut to fit. **Length varies—48" should be enough, but buy more to account for error.

Next, rout a ¼" x ¼" rabbet on each end of each of the tray pieces for the half-lap joinery. Watch out—the router bit has a tendency to fracture and tear out the fibers as you exit the cut, leaving a jagged corner. An easy way to eliminate the blowout is to first make a small cut with a handsaw to define the exit point of the bit.

Next, glue up the trays. It can be tricky to hold the tray together and glue each side at the same time. To make it less of a juggling act, use some painter's tape to temporarily hold the joint together while you apply glue to the other corners.

Before the glue dries, place the tray in clamps snugly, but not fully tightened, so you can check for square. Measure diagonally from corner to corner one way, then the other—the measurements should be the same. If they're off, that means the tray is slightly racked and has to be adjusted. Once you've got it where you want it, slowly and evenly tighten the clamps. Check for square one more time before allowing the glue to set up.

With the glue dry, make sure the top and bottom edges are all flat and flush. If necessary, use a block plane to true

Rabbet. Rout the rabbets on the ends of every tray part. I use a bench hook to hold the work in place and off the bench.

Router setup. Use a ¼" rabbet bit for the joinery. The bit will automatically make a ¼" cut in width because of the bearing size, but the bit still has to be set so it's cutting ¼" down from the base plate.

them up. Cut a ¼" rabbet on the top and bottom edges—you can use the same router setup as you did for the joinery.

The corners of the rabbets will be round. Use a chisel to square these so that the bottoms' corners will seat fully and so the trays nest together in a stack.

Next, cut the ½" plywood bottoms to length and width. Because the rabbets are only ¼" deep, the plywood sits below the sides by ¼"—this lets the bottom register into the top of the tray below. However, the lowest tray's bottom should not project—it should be flush with the side pieces. Use the router with the same bit and depth setting to cut a ¼" rabbet on all four edges of the bottom for the bottom tray. The rabbets on the tray bottom and tray sides will nest together, allowing the bottom to sit flush with the sides. Make sure when routing the outside of the workpiece that you're moving clock wise around the work. Now glue in the plywood bottoms.

Next, reinforce the joinery with some ¼" dowels by drilling three holes in from the sides through each joint. Refer to the drawings for layout—they are ¼" from the ends, and should be evenly spaced. The end grain will want to blow out during this operation—there are a few ways to prevent that from happening. First, place some tape over the corner to reinforce the fibers while drilling. Also, carefully measure and draw the lines where the dowels should be placed to avoid getting too close to the sides of the boards. Lastly, make sure the drill is up to full speed before pushing down into the wood, or it will tend to tear at the fibers instead of cutting them cleanly.

After drilling all the holes, glue in the dowels. To make sure you have the right length of dowel for each hole, keep the dowel long and glue it in one hole at a time. Put glue in the hole and on the end of the dowel rod, then tap the dowel until it's seated. With a flush-cut saw, flush the dowel to the tray surface. Repeat the process for all the tray sides.

GET A HANDLE ON IT

The top divider has a tall handle, and the middle divider has a low handle that sits below its walls. From the drawing on page 44, make full-sized templates for the two dividers and trace them onto the wood. Use a jigsaw or other appropriate saw (such as a bowsaw or bandsaw) to rough out the shape.

Start the finger holds by drilling the outermost holes, then drill several holes in a line between them. Place a

PLAN

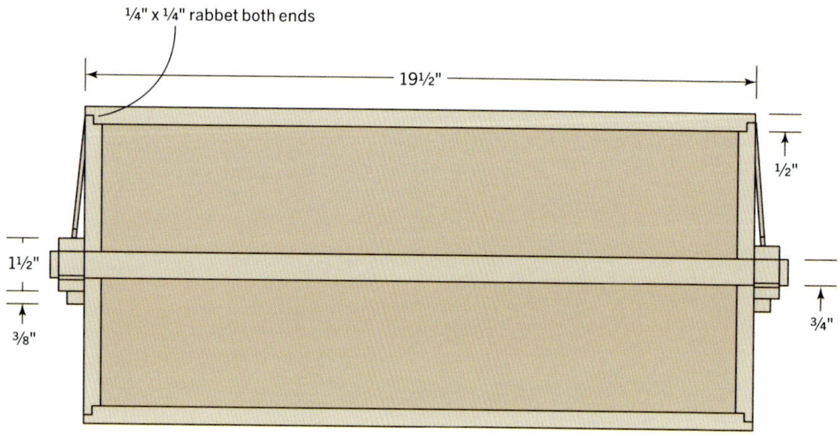

PROFILE

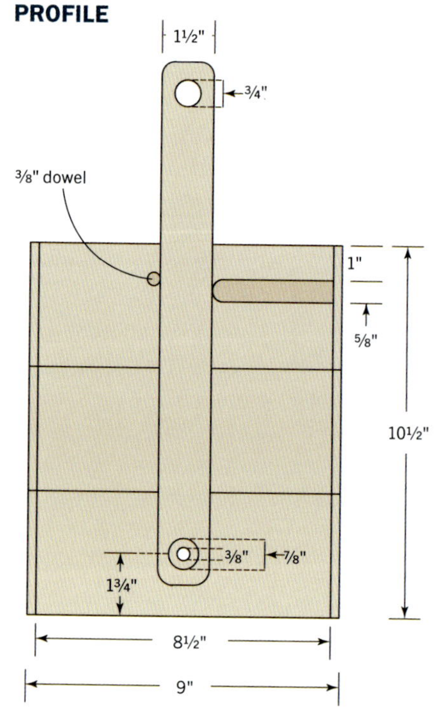

ELEVATION

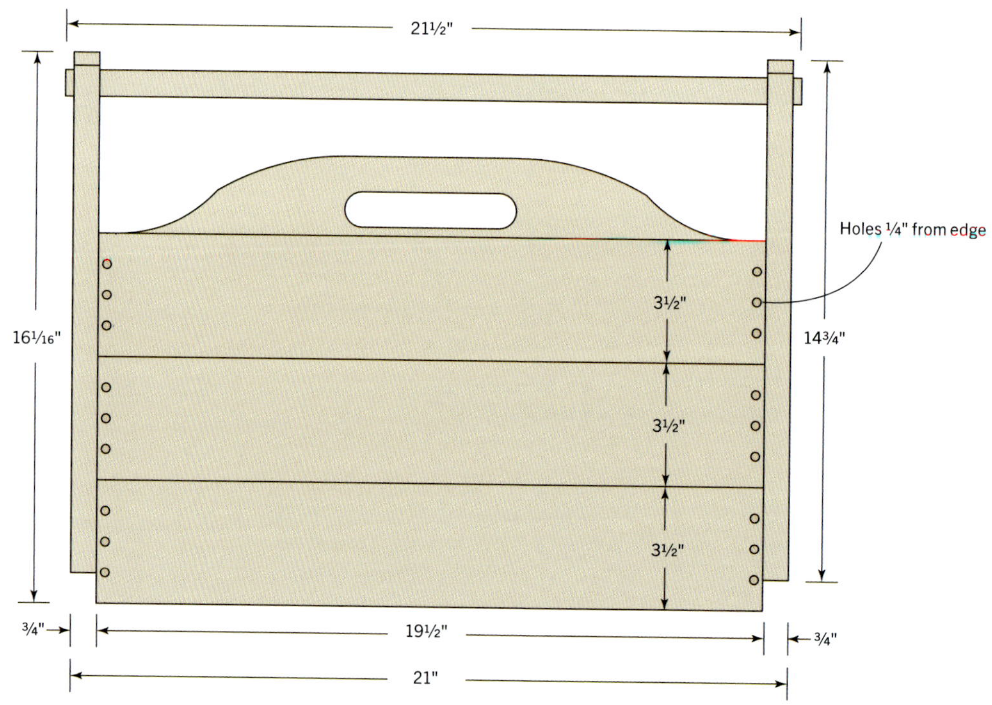

Rout again. Cut a ¼" x ¼" rabbet on the inside of the top and bottom of the trays, after the glue dries. The router bit and setting are the same as for the joints. When routing on the inside of a piece, make sure to move the router clockwise—you should always move the router so the rotation of its bit is against the direction you're moving.

Dowels. Keeping the dowel long assures you'll bottom out on each hole. After applying glue and tapping it home, cut off the excess with a flush-cut saw.

sacrificial piece of wood underneath to prevent drilling into your benchtop. Also, clamp the workpiece to the scrap when drilling—this will prevent blow-out on the other side of the workpiece as the drill bit exits the wood.

Chisel to your layout lines, removing the waste left from drilling. Chop about halfway into the work, then flip the board over and finish the work. This will give you better results because by working from both sides, the back side won't blow out. File and sand to make the divider's curves and finger holds smooth and comfortable to the touch.

To mount the dividers in the tray, find the centers of the tray sides and, with the divider clamped in place, drill ¼" holes from the outside of the tray into the divider. Use ¼" dowel and glue to secure the divider. Both dividers are affixed in the same way.

Before you make the larger exterior handle, make the spring latches and handle stops. The spring latches are made from tongue depressors, which flex to secure the handle vertically. The stops are pieces of dowel that prevent the handle from rotating too far.

TRAY DIVIDERS & HANDLE SUPPORT

One square = 1"

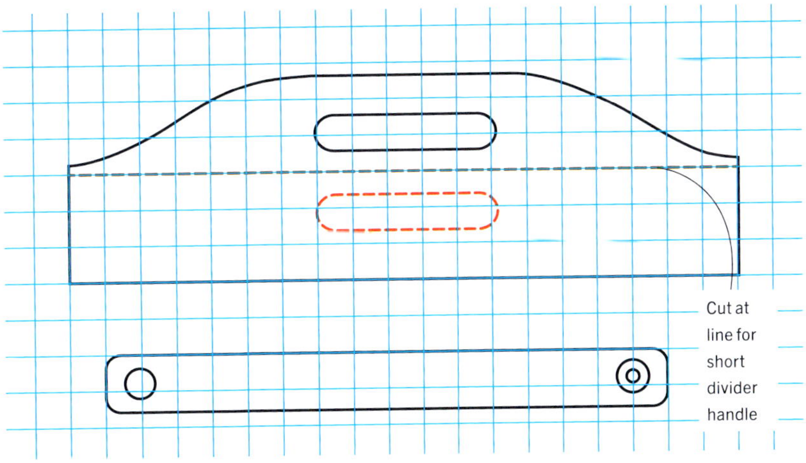

Spring latches. The mortises that hold the spring latches are pared with a chisel held at an angle to form a ramp, which causes them to stand proud. A tongue depressor is just the right size and thickness, but any thin piece of wood will work.

From the plans, lay out the lines for the spring latches on the top tray's sides and use a knife to score deep lines to define each latch's mortise.

With a chisel, pare away the wood between the knife cuts at a gradual slope so the mortise angles upward. Test each latch as you chisel its slot—it should be proud enough to hold the handle back but easy to press down far enough to allow the handle to pass over. Use glue and small brads to secure the spring latches in place.

The handle stops are ⅜" dowels drilled and glued in place. They should be installed so that the handle stops vertically, after passing over the latches.

Now, while the glue for the spring latches and stops is drying, make the main handle. This handle is mounted to the lowest tray by a nut and bolt through the arm and into the tray. The two arms of the handles on either side are connected by a ¾" dowel above the stacking trays.

Cut the arms to length and drill a ⅞" hole part of the way through the bottom of each arm. This will allow the bolt heads to sit below the surface. On the same centers, drill through the arms with a ⅜" bit, and drill a corresponding ⅜" hole into the sides on the lowest tray.

Then drill a ¾" hole all the way through the top of each arm, through which the ¾" dowel will pass to connect the two arms together. Round over and smooth the corners of the arms with a file or sandpaper.

Place a 1½"-long x ¼"-20 bolt and washer through the handle arm on each side. Sandwich another washer between the arms and the sides of the tray, then a washer and nut on the inside of the tray. The nuts might have a tendency to come loose during use, so use Loctite on the bolts before threading the nuts on.

With the bolts tightened and in place, assemble the stacking trays and move the main handle into place. Glue in the ¾" dowel for the main handle. Leave it a little long at this point.

With the dowel in place, but before the glue dries, make the final adjustments on the handle. The arms should be locked in place by the spring latches but still able to pass over them when they're depressed. Adjust the clearance by moving the arms closer or spreading them apart from one another. Once the clearance is correct, let the glue dry, then cut the ends of the dowel flush to the arms. A nail can be driven through the arm into the dowel to further reinforce the joint between the two.

Lastly, sand and finish the parts. I used a simple oil/varnish blend—it applies easily with a rag and gives a soft lustre and a protective finish that isn't too thick. The thin film prevents the finish from chipping or sticking when the trays are stacked together.

Hardware. Attach the handle with the 1½"-long x ¼"-20 bolts. I'm using Loctite to keep the nuts from loosening—once dry, it acts as a mild glue, but can be reversed with some persuasion.

OLD PLANE BIRDHOUSE

You'd be surprised how many woodworking projects start with building a box.

BY CHRISTOPHER SCHWARZ

I've never been a fan of birdhouses. Why welcome something to your yard that wants to poo on your head?

Yet, inspiration works in weird ways. While visiting Maine, I saw an enormous birdhouse that looked like a jointer plane hanging outside Liberty Tool, an ironmonger. I just had to have one to hang above my shop door.

ELEVATION

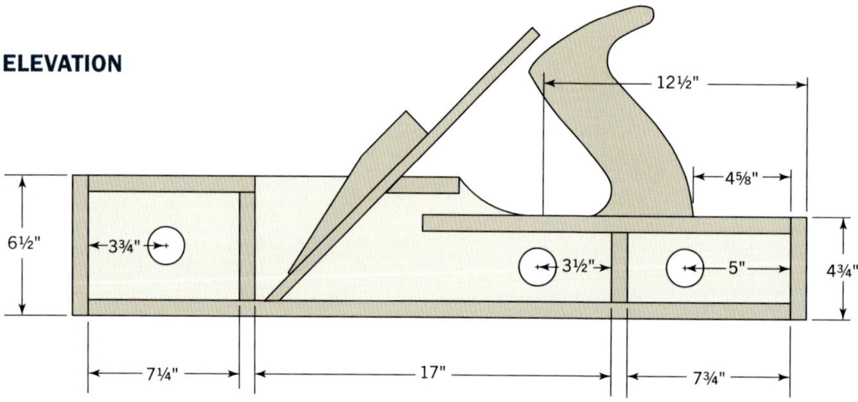

WEDGE & IRON DETAIL

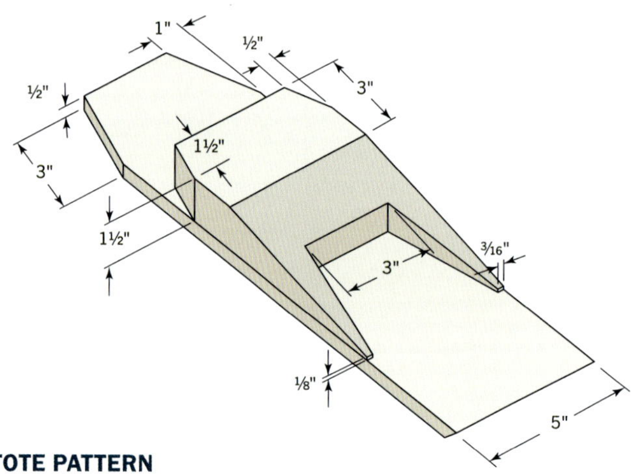

TOTE PATTERN

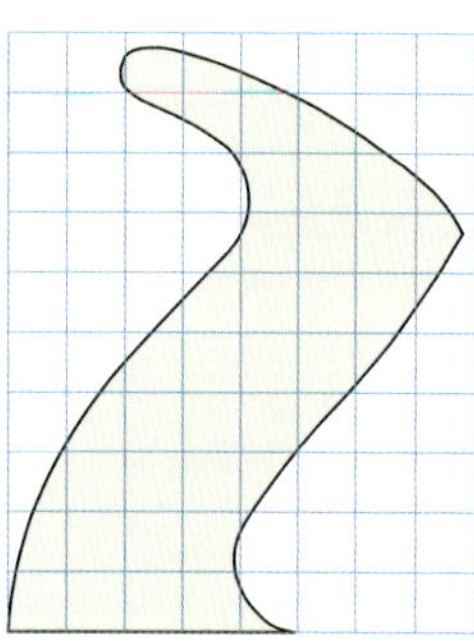

1 grid square = 1"

SIMPLE, QUICK & FUN

This birdhouse is based on a Marples 14" razee jack plane I own. I scaled it up to about 33" long so it would look good above a standard door.

You'll need about 10 to 12 board feet of a weather-resistant wood. I used cypress. And don't forget the waterproof glue and stainless (or galvanized) fasteners.

The whole project takes about three hours, so it also was great therapy for me after coming off of an intense three-month-long project.

Begin by gluing up the wood for the thick wedge and the tote. These pieces are made by gluing two pieces of stock face-to-face. Clamp them up and set them aside for the glue to dry.

NEXT UP: THE SIDEWALLS

After ripping all your parts to width, begin by shaping the two sidewalls. Lay out the razee shape on one sidewall using the drawing as a guide. Cut the shape on the bandsaw and clean it up with a spindle sander. Then use the first sidewall to lay out the pattern for the second.

Cut that one close, then tape the two sidewalls together and shape them simultaneously so they are identical. I used the spindle sander here as well.

ASSEMBLY. WHAT, ALREADY?

Cut the interior parts to size: the toe, heel, top, front of the mouth, frog, divider, and sole. Sand or plane them smooth, then get your nails out.

Glue and nail these seven pieces to the sidewall that will eventually have the entrances for the birds (you'll bore those holes later).

Now shape the tote. Remove the thick piece that you glued up earlier from the clamps and cut it to size using the patterns and drawings provided. Dress it smooth and then screw the tote to the plate for the tote. Glue and nail the finished assembly to the sidewall.

Shape the iron and the wedge using the drawings to guide you. Glue and nail them in place to the sidewall and the frog.

BE BIRD FRIENDLY

Drill some ventilation and drainage holes in the sole and in the top of the plane using a ¼" bit. Then decide what sort of birds you want to attract and drill entrance holes that are based on the species (a quick search on the Internet will call up the hole sizes for a variety of birds). I want to attract Purple Martins, so I drilled my holes at 1⅞" in diameter.

So that the birdhouse is easy to clean, attach the second sidewall to your birdhouse using No. 8 x 1¼" stainless screws.

To hang the birdhouse, I made a French cleat. One half gets screwed to the sidewall. Its mate gets screwed to the house, right above my shop door.

And what about having the birdhouse hanging over my shop door? That seems stupid. Maybe. But perhaps the threat of some loose-boweled birds will prevent my neighbors from pestering me when I'm working in the shop.

CUT LIST & MATERIALS

	NO.	ITEM	DIMENSIONS (INCHES) T	W	L	MATERIAL
☐	2	Sidewalls	¾	6½	33½	Cypress
☐	1	Toe	¾	5	6½	Cypress
☐	1	Top	¾	5	8	Cypress
☐	1	Front of mouth	¾	5	5	Cypress
☐	1	Frog	¾	5	3½	Cypress
☐	1	Plate for tote	¾	5	17½	Cypress
☐	1	Divider	¾	5	3¼	Cypress
☐	1	Heel	¾	5	4¾	Cypress
☐	1	Sole	¾	5	32	Cypress
☐	1	Tote	1½	7½	10	Cypress
☐	1	Wedge	1½	5	9¼	Cypress
☐	1	Iron	½	5	18	Cypress

This plane is hollow. Glue and nail all the interior pieces as shown before you screw the second sidewall in place.

2 CHESTS & STORAGE

THESE LARGER BOXES FIT THE BILL when some serious storage capacity is required. Books, firewood, toys, tools, blankets—what do you have that needs to be put away? Choose the aesthetic of your choice and dive in. From a simple country style brightened with paint to the canted angles of a sea chest, or perhaps the elegant simplicity of the Shaker style or the through joints and exposed ebony of Greene & Greene, there is a design here to complement any home decor. The sturdy pieces within are robust enough to withstand decades of use at the foot of your bed or flanking your front door.

COUNTRY TOOL & TOY CHEST

Nails, glue, and a nice long day in the shop are all it takes.

BY MEGAN FITZPATRICK

This rustic hinged-lid box is a design traditionally used as a basic tool chest, but I thought a scaled-down version would make a great chest for stashing toys (with the addition of a safety hinge) or extra grocery bags in the kitchen. It is adapted from a chest shown in John A. and Joyce C. Nelson's *The Big Book of Weekend Woodworking*.

A TRIP TO THE HOME CENTER

A trip to the home center is the beginning of this country tool and toy chest project, and there I assessed every #2 pine 1x12 in stock. Because I'd decided

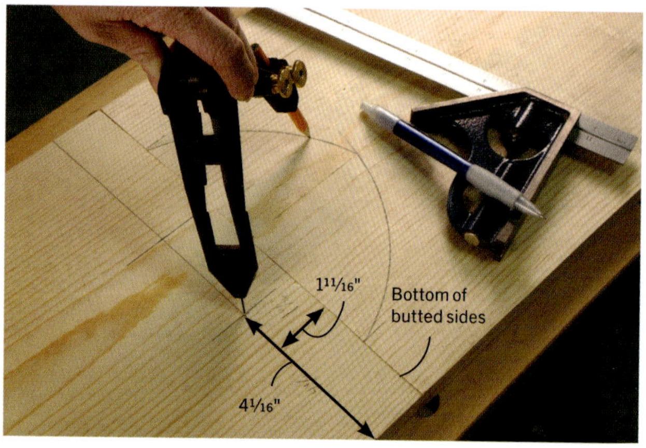

Mark arches. Mark a horizontal line 1$^{11}/_{16}$" from the bottom of each piece, then measure in 4$^{1}/_{16}$" from each of the four sides and mark the intersecting points. These are the four points on which you'll place the point of your compass to mark the arches.

Clean the arches. Clamp the sides together and use a rasp and sandpaper to clean up the arches. Don't worry if they don't match perfectly; because there's 22" between them on the finished chest, minor differences won't be noticeable.

to paint the chest, I wasn't concerned with the grain as much as getting the straightest, flattest boards. While two 8'-long boards would have been enough to construct the chest, I purchased an extra, just in case. I also bought a quart of red paint, 6" strap hinges, and a box of 4d finish nails.

ROUGH CUT THE PIECES

The top and front are the most visible pieces, so I marked these first and rough cut them to length (with a couple inches to spare) using the miter saw. I then selected the next-clearest areas for the sides, then two boards for the back, and finally the bottom. Offcuts were set aside for the battens and cleats.

LAY OUT THE ARCHES

Arched cutouts on the sides dress up the piece a bit. To lay them out, first mark a line on each piece 1$^{11}/_{16}$" up from the bottom, then measure in 4$^{1}/_{16}$" from each long edge on both pieces and mark the intersections. Butt the sides against one another (feet to feet), set the compass to make a 5¼" radius, place the point on each mark, and draw arcs on

PROFILE

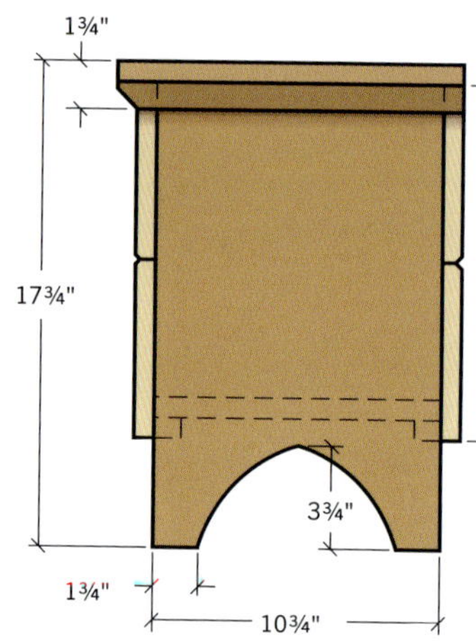

	NO.	ITEM	DIMENSIONS (INCHES)			MATERIAL
			T	W	L	
□	4	Front & backs	¾	6½	22	Pine
□	2	Top	¾	6½	23½	Pine
□	2	Sides	¾	10¾	17	Pine
□	1	Bottom	¾	20½	10¾	Pine
□	2	Battens	¾	1	13	Pine
□		Cleats*	¾	1	72	Pine
□	2	Strap hinges			6	

CUT LIST & MATERIALS

* Cut to fit.

ELEVATION

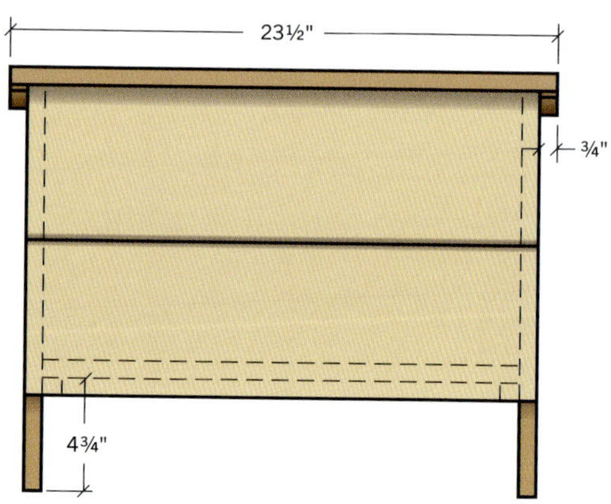

the opposite piece. The two arcs on each piece will intersect at the center of your board, forming the arch apex. Cut out each arch with your jigsaw, then clamp the sides together and clean them up using a rasp and sandpaper.

CHAMFERED PANELS

Because the top, front, and back of the chest are 13" wide and a 1x12 is narrower than that, you have to rip two boards to 6½" wide to make each panel. It's nigh on impossible to cut a glue-ready edge with a jigsaw, so to help disguise any resulting gaps at the seam, I used my block plane to chamfer the adjoining edges.

Now you're ready to assemble the box. Glue and clamp the back boards in place on the sides and drill three ⅛" pilot holes in each board. Drive 4d finish nails into the holes, then repeat this process for the front boards. Leave the nails proud of the surface to avoid dinging the boards with your hammer, then use a nail set to drive them 1⁄16" below the surface.

TOP & BOTTOM

To make the battens, cut two 1" x 13" pieces from your offcuts; trim the front edge at 45° but leave a ¼" flat at the top. To make the top, screw the top pieces to the battens. First snug the two top pieces together on your bench, and lay the battens across either end. Drill countersunk clearance and pilot holes, then attach the battens with #8 x 1½" wood screws.

To make the bottom, first cut your cleats to size and nail them around the inside bottom edge of the chest. Now cut the bottom a hair wider than necessary and use your block plane to trim it to fit. Drop the bottom in place, hang the work over the edge of the workbench so the cleats are supported, then nail the bottom to the cleats from the inside.

WOODWORKING THERAPY

Sand to 120 grit; apply two coats of bright red paint to the outside and a coat of amber shellac to the interior to seal it. After the paint dries, grab a ring of keys and beat the you-know-what out of the box until you get a lot of lovely dings. Take a rasp to the edges, and for good measure, grab your hammer by the head and use the handle end to whomp the top edge a few times. Once the piece looks distressed (and you feel de-stressed) apply a coat of any dark gel stain over the entire thing. Work the stain into the dings, dents and raw edges. Wipe it off, and voilá—a century of age in just minutes. After the stain is completely dry, apply a coat of paste wax.

THE FINISHING TOUCHES

To attach the strap hinges, measure in 4" from the battens on the top, mark the holes with an awl, and drill pilot holes for the screws. The screws that came with the hinges were too long, so we used some we had on hand. You can color the heads black with a permanent marker if you want everything to match. I also attached a length of chain, leaving a few extra loops so the open angle of the top can be easily adjusted.

Make a chamfer. Hold your plane at a 45° angle to the edge of the board, and shave down the length until you're satisfied with the chamfer. The goal is to draw attention to the "seam," so make sure the chamfer is big enough so that paint doesn't overwhelm it.

Pilot & nail. After drilling pilot holes, drive 4d nails and leave them a little proud of the surface.

Put cleats in place. Cut the front and back cleats to size first, then snug the end cleats between them.

STACKING BOOKCASES

Make boxes to fit your books and your space.

BY ROBERT W. LANG

The typical bookcase is a good example of poor design. We make them that way because that's the way we've always made them; almost every plan you see is 12" deep, yet few books require that much space. Most bookcases are heavy and a pain to move. These stacking bookcases solve those problems, and won't take long to build.

Before you begin, assess your library. The three sizes shown here are based on common lumber sizes, and typical sizes of books. If you stay with standard 1x lumber, you won't be able to change the depth, but you can change the height and width.

An inch or two higher than your tallest book is a good inside height, but don't go too wide; beyond 36" and the shelves may begin to sag. Also consider how the parts of the sizes you are planning will fit the available lengths of material; an inch or so of adjustment may save you from buying another board.

GET READY TO RABBET

The individual boxes could be just glued and nailed together, but the rabbet joints shown here will be stronger, and the boxes will be easier to assemble. I used a ⅜"-wide rabbeting bit that uses a ball bearing below the cutter as a guide.

Made to order. Fit the cases to your books to avoid wasting space, lower your material costs, and make moving easy.

Router rules. Clamp the work securely before routing the rabbets and keep the base firmly on the surface.

Nice & square. Clamp a square in the corner to hold the boards in position while you drive and set the nails.

You may find a cheaper version of this bit with a solid piece of steel instead of the bearing. Don't give into the temptation to save a few dollars. The solid guide spins at the same speed as the cutter, fast enough to burn the edges of your wood.

Plan on making at least two passes with the router to reach the final depth. In theory that should be ⅜", but your wood might be a bit thinner or thicker. In reality, the depth is half the thickness of your material.

If you're new to routing rabbets, make a few practice cuts in scrap to get the feel of it. The router will behave differently when you move it in different directions. When you move from left to right, the cutting edge of the bit is moving into the work. This is more efficient and gives you greater control—but when you reach the edge of a board, it tends to break a chip out of the edge.

Moving from right to left is considered backward, and is called "climb-cutting." If you move the router backward into what would normally be the end of a cut before you make the cut, you can prevent blow out. You should only climb-cut for a short distance after the cutter enters the wood.

Keep the base of the router flat on your work while you press the guide bearing against the edge. Be careful at the start and end of a cut that the bearing doesn't go around the corner and on to the adjacent edge.

IN THIS CORNER

Before you put the boxes together, sand the inside surfaces with a random-orbit sander or by hand. It is difficult to sand into the corners after the boxes are assembled. The vertical pieces go outside the horizontal pieces, hiding the end grain when viewed from the side.

Spread a bead of glue on the end-grain surfaces of the sides. Let it soak in for five minutes before applying glue to the other joint surfaces. This allows the glue to soak into the end grain and makes for stronger joints—also called "sizing."

Put the corners together and use clamps to pull them tight. Clamp a speed square (or a square block of wood) in each corner as you nail to keep the entire assembly square. I used 3d finish nails, and set them slightly below the surface of the wood. When the nails are in, the clamps can be removed and you can move on to the next box.

Let the glue dry overnight, and remove any excess wood at the joints with a block plane or a random-orbit sander. When all the corners are flush, sand the outside surfaces and break the sharp corners with sandpaper.

Cut the backs to fit the openings, but finish the bookcases before attaching them permanently. You can hold the backs in place with either 3d finish nails (quick, but be careful with your aim) or #6 x 5⁄8" wood screws.

OFF THE FLOOR

Cut a rabbet along one long edge of the piece for the base before mitering the corners. Size the mitered ends with glue, as was done with the end grain of the rabbets. Assemble the three parts of the base with more glue and nails. Clear packing tape at each corner holds the pieces in position while you nail.

I used clear shellac as the finish, brushing on two coats. Before finishing, I mixed some dust from the collection bag of the sander with a dollop of shellac to make a filler for the nail holes, and any gaps on the edges of the joints. This takes a while to dry, but the price is right, and the color will match the surrounding wood.

After finishing, the boxes are stacked on top of one another and on the base. Drive a couple 1¼" drywall screws from the top of one box into the bottom of the next to keep the assembled bookcase stable.

CUT LIST & MATERIALS

	NO.	ITEM	DIMENSIONS (INCHES) T	W	L	MATERIAL
☐	2	Narrow sides	3⁄4	5½	10¼	1x6 pine
☐	2	Medium sides	3⁄4	7¼	12	1x8 pine
☐	2	Wide sides	3⁄4	9¼	14	1x10 pine
☐	2	Narrow tops & bottoms	3⁄4	5½	23¼	1x6 pine
☐	2	Medium tops & bottoms	3⁄4	7¼	23¼	1x8 pine
☐	2	Wide tops & bottoms	3⁄4	9¼	23¼	1x10 pine
☐	1	Narrow back	¼	9½	23¼	Plywood
☐	1	Medium back	¼	11¼	23¼	Plywood
☐	1	Wide back	¼	13¼	23¼	Plywood
☐	2	Base ends	3⁄4	3½	9⅝	1x4 pine
☐	1	Base front	3⁄4	3½	24¾	1x4 pine

EXPLODED VIEW

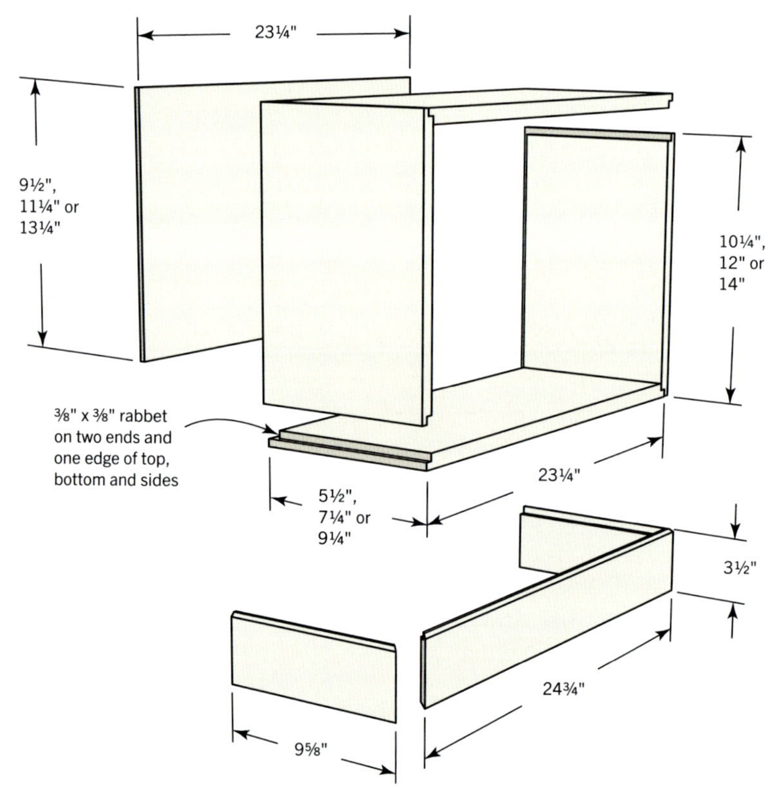

Repurposed. While originally designed to be used to hold firewood and kindling, this Shaker piece also can be pressed into service as a recycling bin.

PLEASANT HILL FIREWOOD BOX

A classic Shaker design with enough curves to make it interesting.

BY CHRISTOPHER SCHWARZ

The buildings at the Shaker Village in Pleasant Hill, Ky., are filled with handy firewood boxes. After a few visits to the colony, I concluded that this example is the best one.

Tucked into a room in the Centre Family Dwelling, this firewood box represents what I like about the Western Shaker furniture styles. This box has a few graceful and unexpected curves, yet it still looks decidedly Shaker.

ELEVATION

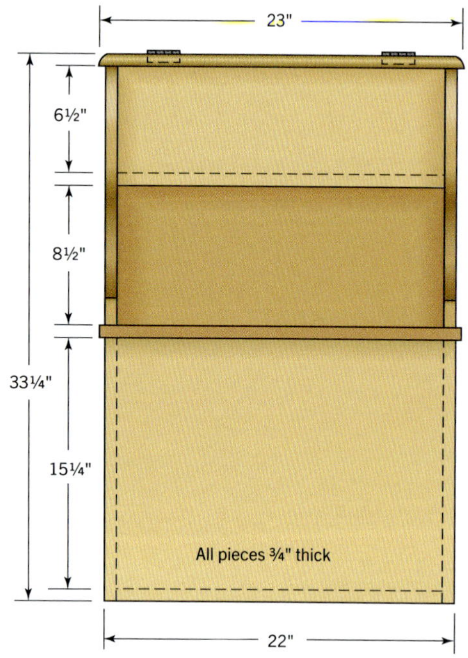

PROFILE

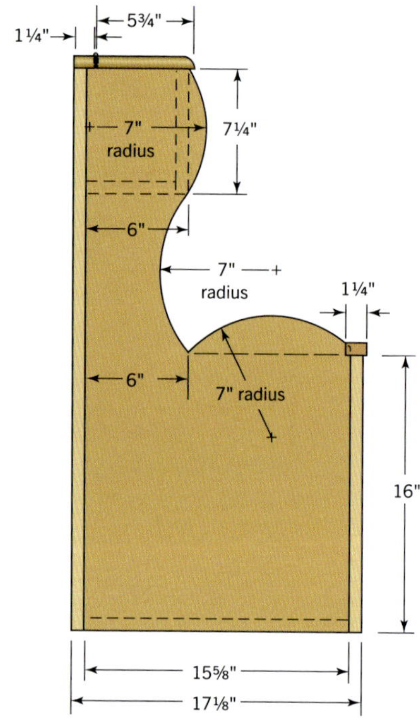

CUT LIST & MATERIALS

	NO.	ITEM	DIMENSIONS (INCHES) T	W	L	MATERIAL	COMMENTS
☐	2	Sides	¾	15⅝	32½	Pine	
☐	1	Front	¾	16	22	Pine	
☐	1	Back	¾	32½	22	Pine	Made from three boards
☐	1	Bottom	¾	15⅝	20½	Pine	
☐	1	Kindling box bottom	¾	5¼	20½	Pine	
☐	1	Kindling box front	¾	7¼	20½	Pine	
☐	1	Kindling box lid	¾	5¾	23	Pine	
☐	1	Hinge rail	¾	1¼	23	Pine	
☐	1	Front edge	¾	1¼	22½	Pine	Notched around sides
☐	2	Hinges					

Building this box is simple. With the exception of the curves on the sides, all the cuts are straight. With the exception of the hinged lid, all the joinery on the box is glue and nails.

The biggest construction challenge is gluing up narrower boards into the panels that make up the box's sides, front, and bottom. I glued these up using pocket screws as clamps.

However, because this project is painted, there's an easier solution at the home center. In the lumber section of the store you'll likely find wide laminated pine panels that are pieced together at a factory from narrow strips. If you purchase this material, you won't have to glue up any panels and can go right to cutting.

The other option is to buy No. 2 common 1 x 12s. I bought five 8'-long 1 x 12s so I could cut around knots. I also bought a small piece of ¼"-thick Masonite. Why? Read on.

MAKE A TEMPLATE

When you're working out a complex design or need to make multiple and identical parts, a full-size template is handy.

With this project, a full-size template helps you get the curves just right and helps you fit the pieces to the hinged kindling box. Plus, if you ever need to make more of these boxes, the template will give you a good head start.

Use the illustration to draw your template on the Masonite using a ruler and a compass. All the curves are a 7" radius, so the layout work is easy. Cut the template to shape using a jigsaw and sand the edges until the template looks good and has smooth edges. If you want to adjust the design, here's your chance to alter it and see how it looks. Glue up all the panels you need and get ready to cut the sides.

CONSTRUCTION

Trace the template's shape on your side pieces and cut them with your jigsaw. Clamp the two sides together and shape the curves with a rasp and sandpaper so the two are identical. Using the side pieces as a guide, determine the actual width of the box's bottom, the width of the bottom of the kindling box, and the width of the front of the kindling box. Cut these three pieces to finished size. Glue and nail them between the sides.

Now work on the front of the box. Cut this panel as close to size as possible—I like to leave it a hair long. Glue and nail the front to the carcase. Trim any overhang with your block plane or 100-grit sandpaper.

Now repeat the same process with the back pieces. I used three horizontal boards for the back. Two of the boards were 1 x 12s. The third one was ripped to fit just right. If you like, you can plane a small chamfer on the back boards' long edges as a decorative detail. This adds a shadow line where the backboards meet one another.

Crosscut the hinge rail and lid at the same time so they are the same length. Your miter saw is an excellent tool for this sort of operation. Screw your hinges to both the hinge rail and the lid. Then glue and nail the hinge rail to the carcase.

The last bit of construction is the box's front edge. I took the difficult route to fit this piece in place. I notched out the underside of the workpiece with a handsaw and chisel so the notches nest neatly over the curve on the sides. You can fit the piece any way your skills or tools allow.

Disassemble the lid and hinges and sand the project up to 150 grit. Break all the sharp edges of the piece by hand with a piece of old sandpaper. The finish is simply three coats of semi-gloss paint. As shown, this piece is a little more barn red than the original. But it is still a red that is consistent with the original Shaker paint recipes. You should, of course, finish yours to suit your decor.

Watch those curves. A full-size template helps in many ways. It allows you to refine the design details, determine the finished sizes of key components and to lay out your cuts.

Variations on a form. The blue chest is the one I built for this article—but let your wood and aesthetics dictate your build. (The yellow chest is by Timothy Henriksen; the green chest is by Ty Black.)

SIX-BOARD CHEST

Use two planks, two days, and two piles of nails to make this age-old form.

BY CHRISTOPHER SCHWARZ

Rip then crosscut. If you rip the molding piece first before crosscutting the front from the back, you will get a nice long piece of straight-grained stock.

Twice as accurate. Ripping the long notches in the ends is easier if you sandwich the two pieces together. Your cut is more likely to remain square.

A plane job. Most of the clean-up of the notches is with a plane. Work to your layout lines and then clean up any excess in the corner.

Six-board chests have been an enduring form of furniture in Western cultures for hundreds of years. And while they differ in their details during different ages, the basic form and the way it is built has been unchanged since the form appeared.

The chest in this article has details I've seen on chests in the 18th and 19th centuries. You can choose different moldings (or omit them), or add carving or a stenciled design to make the chest suit the time period you prefer.

DESIGN WITH THE BOARDS

I built my chest using an 8'-long board and a 12'-long board. Both pine boards were 18½" wide. If you don't have access to wide lumber, feel free to glue up panels to the final width. If your chest is painted, no one will notice.

Because my boards were 18½" wide, I used that fact to help design the chest—there's no need to rip 1" off a wide board or glue on 1". The design of these chests is pretty flexible.

I crosscut the 45" long lid piece from the 8'-long board and set it aside. Why 45"? These chests are typically 32" to 48" long, and 45" was the clearest length of wood I could get from the board. This piece sets the die for the length and depth of the chest.

With the lid cut, I cut the two ends, which determines the height of the chest. These chests typically range from 18" to 27" tall—a good height when it comes to lifting the lid and bending over to get something out of storage. It's not too high or too low.

I cut the ends to 21" long from the remainder of my 8'-long board. This length allowed me to cut around some knots and eliminate some checks on the end of the board. I then set the two ends aside and grabbed my second board.

From this board I cut my front, back, bottom, molding, and battens.

When you cut molding by hand, the best way to do it is to "stick" one long piece of molding and then cut three pieces from that piece. Sticking three pieces of molding is tricky; it's unlikely that you will be able to create exactly the same molding profile on all of them.

Find a piece for the molding that is long enough to wrap around the front and two ends. (Molding on the rear of a chest is unnecessary.) Cut that piece free from your board, then cut the front and back pieces to size. The hard part is done. The remaining stock will be your bottom and lid battens.

JOINERY ON THE ENDS

The first step in creating the joinery for this chest is to deal with the end pieces. They have long notches cut into their long edges to receive the front and back. Not all chests had these notches, but they give you a cleaner look—the outside surfaces of the front, back, and ends are all flush, even at the feet. They also make assembling the chest easier.

Some woodworkers create this notch by scabbing on a small bit at the floor. It seems like a good idea, but I don't have evidence that this was done on histori-

Around the bend. I lay out my ogee on both outside faces of the ends. This helps me make an accurate saw cut because I can peer over the board during the cut to ensure I'm on track.

The hungry chisel. A chisel takes a bigger bite than a router plane, so do as much work as possible with the chisel.

cal chests. Perhaps they didn't do it that way because these chests sat on dirt floors that got wet. And a hide glue joint there would come loose.

Cutting these long notches is easy. Sandwich the boards together and lay out the long notches—each is ⅝" wide and is as long as the front and back pieces are wide.

Pinch the sandwiched boards in your vise and saw the long notches. With the boards still pinched together, use a plane plus a chisel or rasp to true up the notch.

The last task while the ends are sandwiched together is to cut the decorative profile on the bottom of the ends that creates the feet of the chest.

The simplest profile is what antique dealers call the "bootjack"—it's a simple inverted *V* that resembles the tool used for pulling your boots off your feet. This profile is just two lines: two cuts and done. A fancier profile is a half-circle or an ogee. Both of these are laid out with a compass, cut with a frame saw, and smoothed with a rasp.

IN THE HOUSE

The next decision is whether or not to plow dados—housed joints—in the ends that will grasp the bottom board. Here are some pros and cons.

Pros: A dado lets you slide the bottom board in without any battens or glue blocks for support. You don't even need to add glue when sliding the bottom in place.

Cons: Cutting these dados requires extra tools and time.

I always opt for cutting the dados because it makes assembly easier. The first time you cut a long dado, you can nail or clamp a fence to your work to guide your saw. After a dado or two you will realize that the stiffness of the saw's plate is enough to keep you straight.

Saw the walls of your dados, then remove most of the waste with a chisel driven by a mallet. Finish the job with a router plane. The dado is ¼" deep, ⅞" wide, and begins 5" from the bottom of the end pieces.

FRONT & BACK

The front and back pieces are a blank canvas—both for decoration and for joinery. Shallow (¼") rabbets on their ends help make the chest easier to assemble. And you can carve the front, which is typical of 17th-century chests. Or make some simple scratched decoration. Or grain paint it, which was typical in the 19th century.

Let's talk about the joinery first. The reasons to cut the rabbets on the front and back are simple:

1. They help prevent the case from racking after assembly—especially when transporting the chest.

2. They make it easier to assemble the chest yourself. The rabbets lock into the notches in the end pieces. Then you hit a few nails.

3. You can get away with using shorter (and cheaper) nails. If you make this chest using 1"-thick stock, you need 8d nails to assemble the carcase. However, if you cut ¼"-deep rabbets in the front and back pieces, you can use 6d nails instead. If you buy handmade nails, the savings add up.

Cut your ¼"-deep rabbets with a simple rabbet plane or a moving fillister plane. If you are using a simple rabbet plane, first knife a line where you want the shoulder of the rabbet to be. Tilt the plane and put a corner of the tool's sole into the knife line to turn the knife line into a *V*-shaped trench. Then continue to plane until you complete the rabbet. You'll need to tip the plane a little off vertical at first. Then you'll need to tip it vertical.

Cut the rabbets. They don't need to be deep—¼" is perfect—but they need to be consistent in depth so that your carcase is square and everything is flush on the outside. Make the rabbets ⅞" wide to match the thickness of your ends.

With the rabbets complete, clean up the inside surfaces of your ends and the front and back. This is the best time to do this because you are about to nail some things together.

NAIL THE BACK TO THE ENDS

If you've cut rabbets and dados in your parts, here's how to assemble the chest: Nail on the back (add glue if you like). Fit the bottom in the dados. Nail on the front. Then nail the bottom in place all around.

But first, there are some details to consider. The length of your nails should suit the amount of wood that wasn't rabbeted away in the front and the back boards. If you have 1"-thick stock and cut a ¼" rabbet, then you should use 6d nails—8d if you're working in pine. If you have ⅞"-thick stock and cut a ¼"-deep rabbet, you can use 5d nails—6d in pine.

You need a nail with a sizable head for this operation—such as a rosehead. Headless nails or plain brads won't do

EXPLODED VIEW

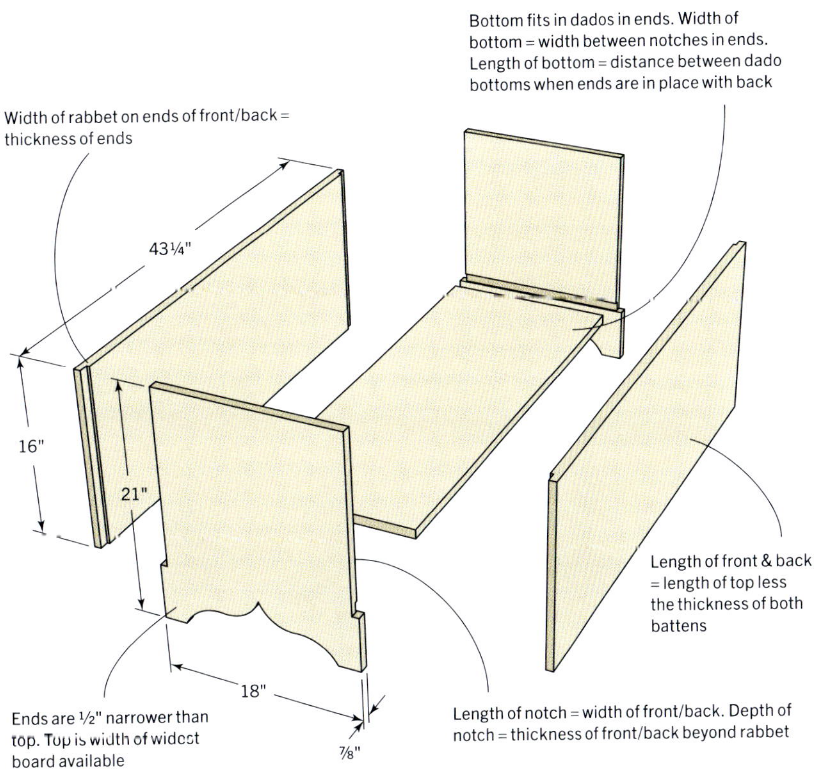

WHY SIX-BOARD CHESTS SURVIVE

When you examine these chests as a builder, they are a bit of a puzzle. The puzzle isn't how they go together, but instead, how they stay that way over time.

These chests disobey many rules of wood movement. The grain on the front and back of the chest is horizontal. The grain on the ends is vertical. The front and back should have split and fallen off. And take a gander at the lid. The grain of the battens that help keep the lid flat and the dust out is 90° to the grain on the lid.

By all rights, the battens should have fallen off, the lid should have split and the whole chest should be a collection of interesting splinters.

Nails—the right nails—allow you to get away with serious crimes of wood movement. Nails are almost always more flexible than screws or dowels. So a nail allows the wood to expand and contract, bending back and forth through the yearly humidity cycles.

Except for hardened masonry nails, I've found that all nails will bend, including wrought nails, cut nails, wire nails, and pneumatic ones. The reason I've always preferred cut nails for making furniture is that they hold better than wire or pneumatic nails. Cut nails are a wedge that—when properly driven—bend and crush the wood fibers in a way that holds the nail fast.

Wire and pneumatic nails aren't wedges, and while they do compress some of the surrounding wood fibers, they are just not in the same league as cut nails (or wrought nails).

Another bonus: A good cut nail will have a rough finish, especially compared to a smooth wire nail. That rough finish also gives the nail some extra bite. This is why many pneumatic nails are coated with a glue that helps them stick in the wood—every little bit helps.

Squaring rabbets. Cross-grain rabbets help square the carcase and line up the pieces during assembly.

Head in. Cut nails with a broad head are the ideal fastener for attaching the front and back to the ends. You can use nails with a smaller head for attaching the bottom.

because they don't have enough holding power. Depending on your stock, you might need to drill a pilot. In some pines and with some nails, you won't. So make a test joint in scrap to find out what holds and what doesn't split. After some experience you will get a feel about what will work.

One last detail: Angle these nails slightly at a small slope—about 5°. And alternate the slopes with every nail. This slope helps keep the front and back wedged onto the ends.

With the back nailed to the ends, cut the bottom board to slide into the dados so the fit is snug and the carcase is square. This is a hand-tool way of approaching the bottom: Create the opening and fit the piece to the opening. If you are machining your bottom, you should be able to hit the length bang-on and nail the bottom onto the ends first.

Usually when I make the bottom with hand tools, it ends up too thick for the dados. Instead of reducing the thickness of the entire bottom, I bevel the underside of the ends—like a raised panel—until the bottom slides in.

I glue the bottom in place all around—then nail it in after assembly. The glue helps here because all the expansion and contraction is in your favor. So take advantage of it.

You don't need to use fancy nails to secure the bottom. Just use 6d or 8d cut finish brads—four through each end and five or six through the front and back. Set these below the surface if they will be covered by molding.

STICKING IT TO THE MOLDING

Skip the molding if you are going for a plain chest. But the molding adds the appearance of a classic plinth—the visual separation between the base section and the not-base section. Surviving pieces were made with and without.

Cut the molding on an 80"-long piece of stock. Then cut the miters. This ensures that your profiles will match at the miters. I profile the molding on a sticking board—a long and flat board with a high fence. I used a ⅜"-square ovolo for this profile.

ON MITERING

The less you fuss about mitering, the better your miters will be. Cut with confidence and calm. I wish someone had told me that when I was starting out.

Wrapping molding around three sides of a carcase is cake compared to making the full 360°. Focus on getting one corner good and tight. Then clamp those two pieces in place on the chest and mark the other corner for its miter.

With both miters cut on the front piece, you can focus on getting the fit tight on the returns (the pieces that "return" down the ends of your chest). I leave the returns long until after everything is glued and nailed in place.

Glue the entire front of the molding to the case. On the returns, glue only the miters and the front one-third of the molding to the ends. Press everything in place for a minute or two. Then drive the brads. The molding should not shift. Set the brads. Then saw the returns flush at the back of the carcase.

ABOUT THE LID

The lid has two important components: its molding profile around the rim and the battens on its underside. The molding profile makes the lid look like some-

CUT LIST & MATERIALS

	NO.	ITEM	DIMENSIONS (INCHES) T	W	L	MATERIAL	COMMENTS
□	1	Lid	⅞	18½	45	Pine	
□	2	Ends	⅞	18	21	Pine	
□	2	Front & back	⅞	16	43¼	Pine	¼ rabbet both ends
□	1	Bottom	⅞	16¾	42	Pine	In dados in ends
□	2	Battens	⅞	⅞	18½	Pine	
□	2	Hinges					
□	1	Strap					Leather

Miter slices. Here is how you miter your stuck molding. By sawing close to your line you can make the grain and profile match around the corner perfectly.

thing more sophisticated than leftover siding. The battens keep the lid flat—if you attach them correctly.

First, cut the molding profile on the two ends and the front of the lid. It can be almost any profile you have on hand. I have a larger ovolo plane (½" wide) that looks like a lot of other lids for chests that I've seen. Cut the profile on the ends first, then on the front edge. This allows you to erase any splintering from working across the grain.

The battens on the ends of the lid keep it flat. Nailing the battens to the lid isn't enough—the battens will fall off when the top moves. Gluing the battens won't do. Nailing and gluing is better, but the lid's movement is still stronger than that joint.

You have two choices: old school and modern. The modern approach is to screw the battens to the underside of the lid and ream out the pilot holes for the screws so the lid can move. The other approach is to drive nails through the battens and the lid so that the tips protrude through the molding, then bend the tips back into the molding.

Choose nails that protrude about ½" beyond the molding. Then turn the tip of the nail over like a fishhook and drive it back into the molding. This secures the batten to the lid and keeps the lid fairly flat.

HINGE & FINISH

There are a variety of ways to attach the hinges to the carcase and lid. Snipe hinges are an old solution (you can make your own using 2" cotter pins).

These chests were typically painted on the outside and left bare inside. The paint highlights the form of the chest and obscures the distracting cross-grain aspects of the form.

What paint you choose should be based on:

■ Do you hate strong smells? Use latex.

■ Does the paint need to be bomb-proof? Consider oil-based.

■ Do you want a traditional look? Use commercial milk paint.

■ Are you a glutton for punishment? Make your own paint.

I use commercial "milk" paint. I know it's not historically accurate, but it does give me a look I like. Plus it is quite durable and fairly low on the toxicity scale. I apply two coats of paint and sand between the coats with a 320-grit sanding sponge.

After building several of these chests, both by myself and with friends, I found that the process became faster and faster (two days is almost a luxurious amount of time). In fact, it took longer to type this explanation of building the piece than to actually make it.

Bent over. Clenching the nails back into the molding hooks the battens to the underside of the lid.

Finish up. Hinges of your choice and a leather strap to hold the lid complete this simple chest.

While the angled panels make this chest look difficult to build, the construction is actually quite simple. It's a great introduction to angled work for the beginning woodworker.

A SIMPLE SEA CHEST

Whether you're a polished skipper or a certified landlubber, you'll find many reasons to build this canted-side sea chest.

BY GLEN HUEY

If you were a sailor who sailed deep waters prior to 1870, you packed your belongings into a sea chest. (Coastal sailors, those who returned to port often, used a sea bag.) Sea chests—banned by the United States Navy in 1870 due to the lack of space for each sailor to have his own chest—are simply six-board chests.

Designs range from straight-sided chests, to those that are canted or angled on the front, to examples with both the front and back canted.

Why are the sides angled? That was to help protect sailor's shins from knocking the lid as the ship rocked with the swells of the water.

While most sea chests feature dovetailed corners, we've simplified the construction of this example and maintained the design to build a chest with basic joinery.

SET SAIL ON THE PROJECT

To begin construction, mill the four case panels—both ends, the front, and

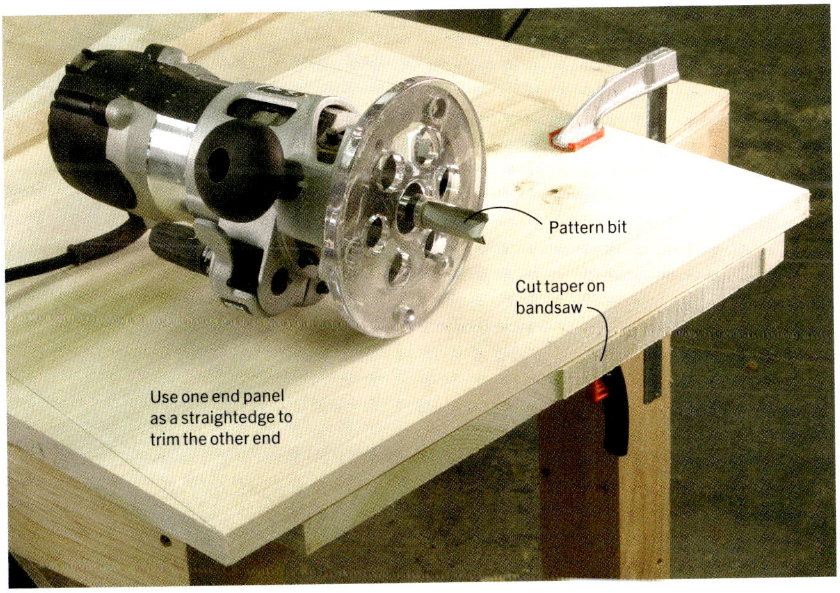

A router with a pattern bit is a perfect method of obtaining a square, straight edge—given you start with a straightedge as your pattern.

Transfer the angle of the canted front and back from the chest to the table saw with a bevel gauge. Set the angle dead-on to make the cuts accurate.

back—to size and thickness. With the two ends front and center, establish the chest's shin-saving angle. Mark a point along the top edge of the panel that's 2" in from each end. Next, use a straightedge to draw a line connecting those points with the nearest bottom-edge corner. Bingo: the angle is set.

Because this type of cut doesn't work well at the table saw, I think it's best to use an alternative method. Cut close to the line at your bandsaw then finish the cut with a router and a pattern bit. Use the bottom edge of the opposite end panel for a simple straightedge.

The most important measurement you'll use in building this chest is that angle created on the end panels. Use a bevel gauge to find the angle.

Take the gauge to your table saw and tilt the blade to match the setting of the bevel gauge and remember that degree setting.

With the blade tilted, cut one edge of the previously squared front and back panels with the face side up. You just want to remove material to create the bevel, not much more. Next, move the fence closer to the blade, flip the face side down, and cut the opposite edge of the panels. If you cut both panels at the same setting, you ensure the front and back panels match in width.

Both ends of the front and back panels receive rabbets on the interior face. Install a dado stack at its widest setting in the table saw, attach an auxiliary fence, and bury some of the stack into the fence, but leave ¾" exposed. Set the blade height to ½" then run the panels against the auxiliary fence to cut the four rabbets.

FIT, TRIM & NAIL

When the angle is cut on the edges of the front and back panels, the widths of the pieces diminish slightly. As a result, the ends need to be trimmed. Position one end to either the front or back panel then mark the amount needed to restore the match. Trim the ends at the table saw.

Assemble the box one end at a time. With the pieces aligned and in position, remove one end panel then add glue

Nibble. Drawing pencil lines along the board's edge allows you to sneak up on the cut without removing too much material. Due to the angle of the saw blade, you'll nibble the bottom of the edge and work your way to the top. When the pencil lines are gone, you're at the top edge.

Trim. Look for ⅛" shrinkage once the front and back are trimmed to match the angle of the end pieces. The ends need to be trimmed to an exact match.

Clamp for nailing. Thanks to the rabbeted corners, clamps positioned at the top and bottom hold the case square and are away from the corners to make nailing the corners a simple task.

along the entire rabbet—the grain on all panels runs the same direction so there are no concerns with cross-grain construction. Replace the end panel on the box then add clamps.

Tap the ends to make sure they seat into the glue and are tight to the other panels, then you're ready to nail the joint together. That's right, nail. Building a chest couldn't get much easier.

There is a secret to nailing this chest without incident. If you're using reproduction cut nails, it's necessary to align the widest part of the nail with the grain direction of the wood. That, along with drilling a proper-sized pilot hole, keeps the grain from splitting. Nail both corners of the first end, then repeat the steps for the second end.

BOARD NUMBER FIVE

The fifth board of this six-board chest is the bottom. The bottom of the chest is actually a series of three boards

Don't split. A guaranteed way to split the grain of the front and back panels is to attempt to install a reproduction fine finish nail into your chest with the head of the nail positioned across the grain.

Keep in place. The outer bottom pieces cannot lift up due to the angle of the chest. To keep the opposite edge in position, make sure the rabbets are cut into the face of the bottom pieces and get the center board rabbeted to fit.

END VIEW SECTION

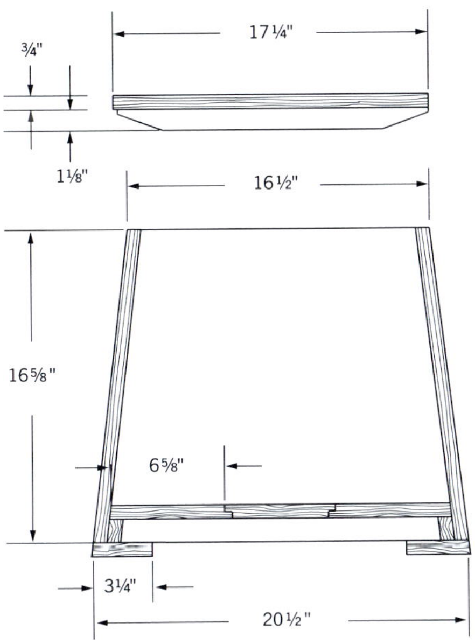

FRONT VIEW

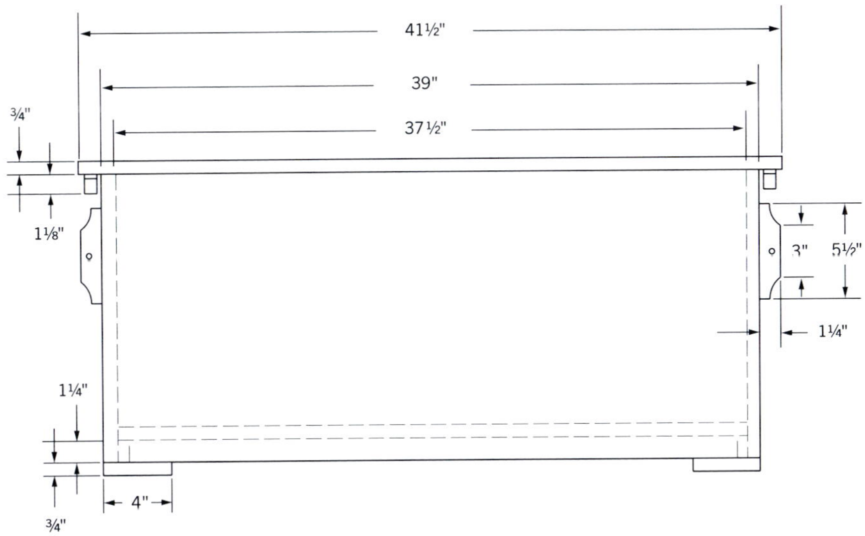

affixed onto a rim that encompasses the entire box. Begin by milling the long rim pieces to size, then angle-cut their edges just as you did on the front and back panels—again the angle measurements are important.

The long rim pieces are fit to the front and back on the interior of the chest, flush with the bottom edge. The end cuts are square and made with a miter saw. I used a thin bead of glue and nails to attach the rim.

Because the width of the long rim pieces change when cut, as did the panels, you also have to adjust the width of the short rim pieces. The short rim pieces run from side to side, between the installed long rims. Make the end cuts at a miter saw with the blade angled to the correct setting. The cut is across the end, not along the edge. Add glue, then nail the short rims to the chest.

Mill the three pieces for the bottom to thickness. Then, at the table saw, create one angled edge with the blade once again set to match the bevel gauge.

The opposite edges of the two outside bottom boards receive rabbets. It's important to cut the rabbets on the top

CUT LIST & MATERIALS

	NO.	PART	SIZES (INCHES)			MATERIAL
			T	W	L	
☐	2	Front & back panels	¾	16¾†	39	Poplar
☐	2	End panels	¾	16¾†	20	Poplar
☐	1	Lid	¾	17¼	41½	QSWO*
☐	2	Battens	¾	1⅛	17	QSWO*
☐	2	Long rims	¾	1¼†	38†	Poplar
☐	2	Short rims	¾	1¼†	18†	Poplar
☐	4	Feet	¾	3¼	4	Poplar
☐	2	Outer bottom	¾	7	37½	Poplar
☐	1	Center bottom	¾	5¼†	37½	Poplar
☐	2	Cleats	⅞	1½	5½	QSWO*
☐	2	Unequal strap hinges			8 x 3	

* Quartersawn white oak; † Trim to fit

Add feet. Attach feet to the base of the chest to raise the bottom off a floor (or a ship's deck). These feet are cut to the appropriate angle to match the slope of the front and rear faces.

Use what you need. Nowhere is it written you have to use the entire router bit. Use only a portion of the roundover router bit to create the edge profile for the chest.

Avoid stress. Seasonal-adjustment stress is relieved by mounting the battens with pan-head screws through slightly oversized holes. Drill a pilot hole, then add wax to the screw to reduce chances of splitting the lid.

edge of the boards, or on the narrow face. The angled edge has to fit against the chest sides with the rabbeted edge showing as you peer into the chest.

Cut the outside bottom boards to length, then position them inside the case. Push the pieces against the front and back of the chest, then measure the distance between the two rabbeted edges. The distance measured is the width of the third board that completes the bottom.

Once that piece is sized at the table saw, create rabbets that match those on the outside boards. Cut the middle board to length, then slip it into the chest. A couple screws at each end of the middle board keep the bottom in place—but it wouldn't hurt to add a fastener to the outside boards too.

ADD A LITTLE LIFT

This chest is raised off the floor with four feet. One edge of the feet, the 4" edge, is cut at an angle to match the chest, while the edges facing the ends are square cut.

Mill the stock to size, then cut the matching angle at the table saw. Next, move to the miter saw and cut four pieces to the final size (3¼").

With the chest on its top, position the feet so both show edges are flush with the chest. Drill countersinks into the feet, two into the front/back panels, and one into the end panels.

To add a nice touch to an area of the chest that's seldom seen, clip the interior corner of the feet. Position the foot to the chest, mark the foot at the inside edge of the rim pieces, then use a miter saw to cut between those two points.

Add a thin bead of glue to the foot, orient the foot to the chest, and attach the two using #8 x 1¼" wood screws.

LAST BUT NOT LEAST

The base of the chest is finished in paint, but I chose to stain the lid, battens, and cleats. Mill the material necessary for the stained parts, then size the lid according to the cut sheet.

Work begins at a router table. The edge profile is not a true roundover, but it is made with a ½" roundover router bit. Adjust the bit height so only the upper portion is being used (see photo top center.) Shape the ends first, then the front edge. Flip the panel and repeat on the opposite face to finish the complete profile. The rear edge of the top panels is left square.

Battens, found on most sea chests, are a snap to create. Cut the stock to size, then lay out the cut lines. Mark the halfway point on both ends of each batten (¾"), move in along the bottom edge, and place a mark at 2½". Connect those points. Cut close to the lines with a bandsaw, then smooth to the lines with a sander.

The battens are screwed to the lid. Make sure your screws hold firm, but be careful—if you drive the screw too far, the face of the lid will be damaged.

Use a drill press to countersink three ⅝" holes (one centered along the length and one 1¼" in from each end). Set your depth stop at ¾" off the drill press table—leaving the material that thickness works perfectly for #12 x 1¼" pan-head screws. Once the countersink is drilled, continue through the batten with a ¼" drill bit.

Position the battens just inside the molded edge, ¼" from the outside edge of the chest. Add a bead of glue along

Pilot. Position the cleat to the case sides, mark for screws, then drill small pilot holes from the outside in. This establishes a precise interior location for countersink holes.

Refine the hinge. The softer metal of the strap hinges affords an opportunity to bend the hinge to a "proper" design for trunks and chest. Matching screws to the hardware improves the aesthetics of the project.

the front 4" and use clamps to hold the pieces firm. Drill a small pilot hole prior to installing the screws, cinching them tight.

The ¼" hole is a larger diameter than the screw, which affords a small amount of compensation for wood movement while the glue at the front forces movement toward the rear of the top.

Unequal strap hinges used for chests are most often crooked to fit inside the chest back and under the lid. The hinges selected for this chest require some simple bends to fit that profile. These bends can be easily accomplished with a vise and hammer. Install the hinges but remove them prior to finishing the chest.

GET A HANDLE ON IT

Handles on many antique sea chests are considered works of art. The cleat is only part of the story for top-quality chests. A second important aspect is the rope pulls or "beckets." Many beckets are very fancy. This chest is basic and the beckets are grommet style—rope tied through holes in the cleat.

The cleats, one on each side of the chest, begin as pieces that are as thick as can be garnered from rough 4/4 stock, or ⅞" at minimum. Arcs cut at the ends of each cleat are decorative. To match the look on this chest, remove ¾" of the width and 1½" along the length at each end. Make the cut at a bandsaw, then smooth the area with a spindle sander.

The beckets are attached through two holes drilled into each cleat. Draw a line across each cleat that's centered from top to bottom, then equally space and drill two 5⁄16" holes along that line. Slightly oversized holes allow easy installation of the ¼" rope.

The cleats are attached with two screws through the interior of the chest. Position the cleats prior to any finishing steps, then drill and countersink holes for the screws. Install the cleats, but remove them prior to finishing the chest. Note which side of the chest each cleat fits so installation after finishing is less frustrating.

When the chest is completely finished and the cleats are once again installed, on goes the rope or beckets. Start with a 27" piece of rope, tie one end in a figure-eight knot, then slide the opposite end into the rear hole of the cleat. Loop the piece through the front hole to form a handle, and tie a second knot to secure the handle near the end. Each pull of the beckets squeezes the knots tighter.

ABOUT THE FINISH

Sand the entire project with 150-grit sandpaper and prepare to paint and stain. The finish on this sea chest base is a painted crackle finish. The crackle effect adds age to any project as well as an interesting look. A few products available at most home-center stores are all you'll need.

The stain finish is a coat of Olympic Interior "Special Walnut" oil-based stain with a layer of Watco "Dark Walnut" Danish oil, topped with a layer of shellac.

DANISH MODERN CAMPAIGN CHEST

Built to move (and to last), this piece blends classic proportions and clean lines.

BY CHRISTOPHER SCHWARZ

When the British Empire began taking over the world in the 18th century, one vexing problem at its tropical holdings was the monsoon season. When it hit, applied carvings and ornaments fell off the furniture, or the glue was consumed by insects.

Undeterred, the Empire developed a new kind of robust and unadorned furniture—what we now call campaign furniture—to hold the undergarments, brandy, and books of the Empire's subjects in all four corners of the globe.

What is most interesting about campaign furniture is how it inspired many early 20th-century makers to create Danish Modern and other contemporary styles that were extremely well made but unencumbered by ornament.

This chest of drawers explores that link between the 19th and 20th centuries by starting with pre-Industrial proportions for chests of drawers and stripping away everything that is not needed.

Like most campaign chests, all the pulls and lifts are flush to the carcase, though in this case they are cutouts backed with darkened brass. Also like campaign chests, the entire thing breaks apart to be moved easily to a new apartment (or tent in the desert). But unlike 19th-century campaign furniture, this chest embraces contemporary joinery to make the chest a cinch to build.

HOW IT GOES TOGETHER

The two carcases are joined with Festool Dominos, though almost any other carcase joint will do. I've built many traditional campaign chests with full-blind rabbeted dovetails. You might also consider biscuits or dowels.

The exterior panels are made of quartersawn white oak. The interior panels are pine or pine with a strip of white oak glued on the front edge. This construction saves on weight and expense. The backs of the carcases are captured in grooves in the tops, bottoms, and end pieces. Once the two carcases are assembled, they stack on top of one another. To keep the top carcase from sliding around, it rests on dowels sticking up from the bottom carcase. Gravity does most of the work.

The plinth, or base, is simple. Two strips of wood are screwed to the underside of the lower carcase. The four legs—tapered octagons—are friction fit into holes bored in the strips.

Like the case, the drawers are also built using Dominos, with the drawer bottoms captured in grooves. All in all, it's a surprisingly quick project to build, especially if you own a Festool Domino. Begin by gluing up any panels you might need for the tops, bottoms, ends, and dividers in the cases. Cut these casework pieces to finished size and prepare to cut the grooves for the backs.

GROOVES: STOPPED & THROUGH

The grooves that hold the back are ½" wide and ¼" deep. The grooves in the end pieces run through from end to end

All the way through. The through-grooves in the ends of the carcase are easy to make with a router and a fence to guide the tool's base.

Stop here. When routing the grooves in the top and bottom pieces, you have to make sure the grooves do not go through the ends of the boards. I do this by eye because all this will be hidden in the glued-up carcase.

Into the end. Though this is a modern joint, traditional workholding is still my favorite way to keep the parts clamped to the bench.

without stopping. The grooves in the top and bottom pieces, however, stop about ⅜" from the ends so the grooves don't show when the case is assembled.

As you study the cutlist and drawings, you'll see a subtle difference in the way the backs go into the grooves in the top carcase versus the bottom carcase.

CUT LIST & MATERIALS

	NO.	ITEM	DIMENSIONS (INCHES)			MATERIAL
			T	W	L	
TOP CASE						
☐	1	Top	¾	17	36	Oak
☐	2	Ends	¾	17	16½	Oak
☐	1	Bottom	¾	15½	34½	Pine
☐	1	Horizontal divider	¾	16¼	34½	Pine, oak edge
☐	1	Vertical divider	¾	16¼	7⅞	Pine, oak edge
☐	1	Back	½	16¾	35	Pine
LOWER CASE						
☐	2	Top & bottom	¾	17	36	Oak
☐	2	Ends	¾	17	16½	Oak
☐	1	Horizontal divider	¾	16¼	34½	Pine, oak edge
☐	1	Back	½	17	35	Pine
☐	2	Dowels	1-dia.		⅞	Oak
TOP DRAWERS						
☐	2	Fronts	¾	7⅞	16⅞	Oak
☐	4	Sides	½	7⅞	15	Poplar
☐	2	Backs	½	6⅞	16⅜	Poplar
☐	2	Bottoms	½	14¾	16⅜	Poplar
SECOND DRAWER						
☐	1	Front	¾	7⅞	34½	Oak
☐	2	Sides	½	7⅛	15	Poplar
☐	1	Back	½	6⅛	34	Poplar
☐	1	Bottom	½	14¾	34	Poplar
BOTTOM DRAWERS						
☐	2	Fronts	¾	7⅞	34½	Oak
☐	4	Sides	½	7⅞	15	Poplar
☐	2	Backs	½	6⅞	34	Poplar
☐	2	Bottoms	½	14¾	34	Poplar
PLINTH						
☐	2	Base pieces	1⅜	3	33	Pine
☐	4	Legs	1½	1½	6½	Oak
SUPPLIES						
☐	8	Cutout backplates	1⁄16			Brass

In the top carcase, the back can be slid into the carcase after it is glued up because the bottom of that carcase is a little narrower. On the other hand, the back for the bottom carcase is captured all around and must be inserted during assembly. The reason for this difference is cosmetic and prevents an odd notch from appearing at the back of the bottom carcase.

I usually cut grooves with a plow plane, but because these grooves are stopped, I turned to my plunge router. I chucked a ½" straight bit in the collet and clamped a fence to the work to guide the router's base.

The through-grooves in the end pieces are simple to make. But you have to pay attention when cutting the stopped grooves in the top and bottom pieces. It's easy to overshoot and groove the boards all the way through.

Before diving into the Domino joinery, it's best to make the half-moon cutouts in the ends that serve as chest lifts. Because there are 12 of these cutouts, I made a template from MDF to both mark and rout the cutouts. The top of the cutout shape is a straight line 4" long. The curve below is a 2" radius.

Use the template to mark the four cutouts in the end pieces. Then remove as much waste as possible with a Forstner or other drill bit. Then clamp the template to your end piece and use a pattern-cutting bit in your router to finish the shape.

DOMINO JOINERY

Though I use traditional hand-cut joinery for most things, I cannot deny the Domino is a legitimate way to make excellent joints. I bought the machine for production work when it was first introduced and have been impressed with it. It is superior to a dowel or biscuit machine and produces a robust loose-tenon joint with ease.

Mark & bore. Use your template to trace the half-moon shape on the work. Remove as much waste as possible with a drill bit.

Then rout. Use the template to guide a router with a pattern-cutting bit to complete the shape.

For this piece, I used 5 mm x 30 mm Dominos to join the tops, bottoms, ends, and the dividers between the drawers. I recommend at least five or six Dominos per joint.

Note the trickiness when it comes to attaching the bottom panel of the top carcase. It's ¾" narrower than both the top panel and horizontal drawer divider. And it is captured between the end pieces. This small complication allows the finished piece to have only one horizontal drawer divider showing between the top and bottom cases. (See the "Detail: Second Drawer" illustration on p. 77.)

The trickiest part of the joinery for the case is the vertical divider between the two top drawers. The first hurdle is getting the drawer divider the correct height. Here's how: Once the horizontal divider is mortised, clamp up the carcase without glue. Place the overtall vertical drawer divider up against the end piece and use it as a ruler to mark the finished height with a knife. Saw and shoot the divider to finished height.

The last major operation before gluing the carcase parts together is to relieve the interior of the half-moon handle cutouts. This relief, which is made with a cove bit in a router, gives a place for your fingers to go when lifting the carcase.

ASSEMBLE THE CARCASES

Before assembly, use a smoothing plane to remove all the ugly machine marks from the panels.

While I used modern joints on this piece, I opted for traditional glue. Liquid hide glue is an outstanding glue for Domino, biscuit, or dowel joinery. Unlike yellow glue, hide glue doesn't tend to swell and lock your joints—it's much more of a lubricant. It also sets up slowly (which is great when you work by yourself) and it is reversible (which is great when you mess things up by yourself).

Assemble the carcases by working from the center out. Glue the horizontal dividers to the ends and clamp them together. Then add any other dividers, plus the top and bottom. After clamping everything together, check each carcase to ensure it is square.

The only big difference between the assembly process for the top and bottom carcases is that the top carcase has a vertical drawer divider (the bottom carcase doesn't). And with the bottom carcase, you'll need to insert the cab-

Divider trick. Use the drawer dividers as a fence to guide the Domino when cutting the mortises in the end pieces (top). Then turn the machine 90° and use the same layout marks to make the mortises in the drawer divider (bottom).

PLAN SECTION

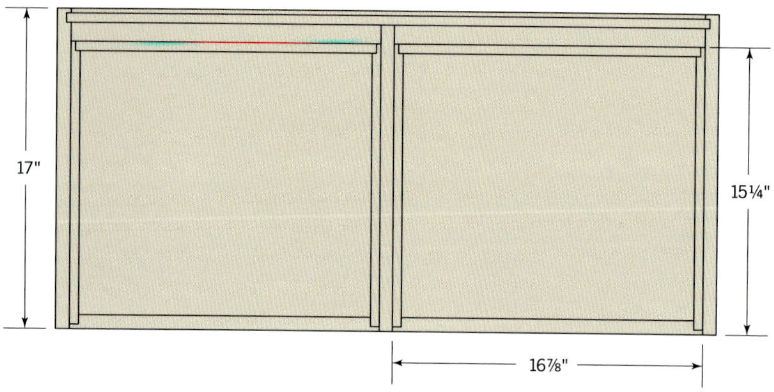

inet back in place during assembly (as mentioned earlier). So don't forget to do that.

After the glue has cured, remove the clamps. Slide the ½"-thick back into the top case and nail the backs to the carcase members. I used 4d die-forged nails, which hold tenaciously but let the wood move without cracking.

DOMINO DRAWERS

I think it's been about 15 years since I made a drawer without using dovetails. But after much thought, I concluded that a drawer made with Dominos could be incredibly strong. And I came up with an easy method that requires little layout or tricky cuts.

PROFILE SECTION

ELEVATION

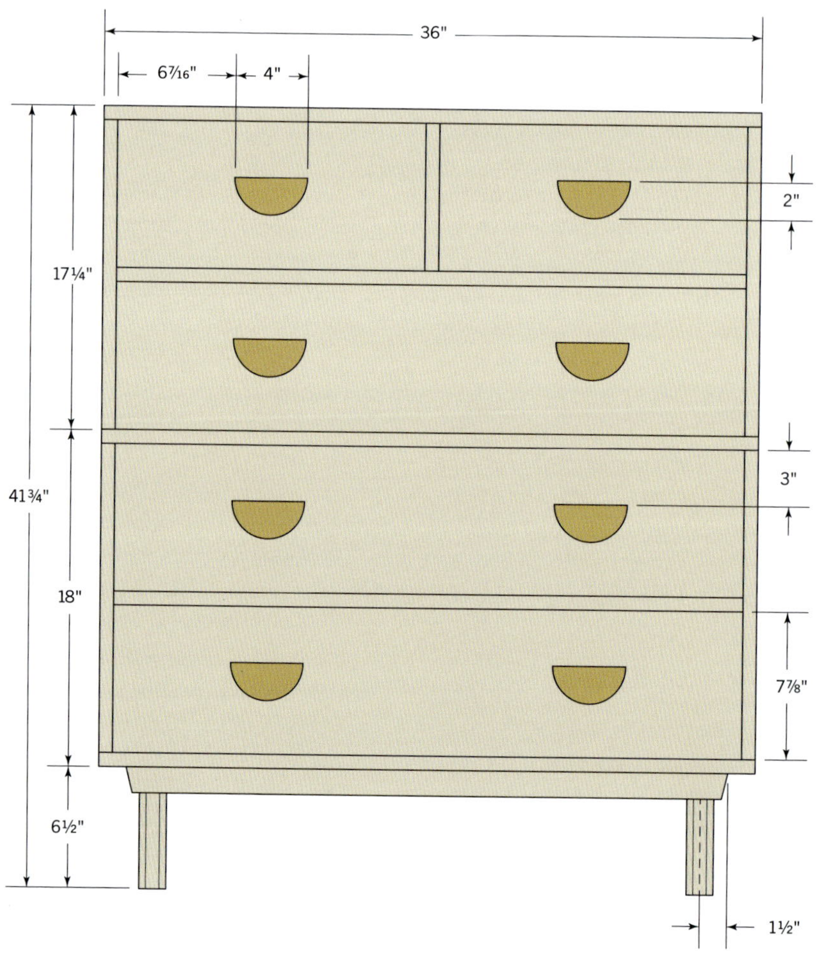

Here's an overview: It begins by making a simple rabbeted drawer and gluing it together. The drawer front has ½" x ½" rabbets at both ends. The ½"-thick drawer sides have ½" x ¼" rabbets cut on their back ends. Then, to hold the ½"-thick bottom, make ½" x ¼"-deep grooves in the drawer sides and drawer front.

Glue up the drawer. After the glue is dry, use the Domino to cut 5 mm x 28 mm-deep mortises through the drawer sides and into the drawer front and drawer back. Glue in 5 mm x 30 mm Dominos and cut them flush after the glue dries.

This creates, for lack of a better word, a through-Domino joint, which works much like a "pin and crescent" joint—also called a Knapp joint.

First cut all your drawer parts to finished size and check them against your glued-up carcases to ensure they fit into their drawer openings. Make the cutouts for the drawer pulls and rout the coved relief on the inside—just like you did on the ends of the carcases. Then cut all the rabbets and grooves for all of the pieces. Then assemble the drawers with glue and clamps.

After the glue has cured, level the joints and bevel off the top rear corner of the drawer sides. This makes it easier to insert the drawer into the carcase. Note also that the drawer back isn't as tall as the drawer sides. This detail makes the drawer easier to close.

Now fit the drawer bottoms into the drawers and secure them with a couple 4d nails through the bottom and into the drawer back.

CUT THE DRAWER MORTISES

With the drawers assembled, you can cut the 5 mm x 28 mm mortises for the Dominos in the finished assemblies. I used four Dominos at each front corner of the drawers with three at each back corner.

DETAIL: SECOND DRAWER

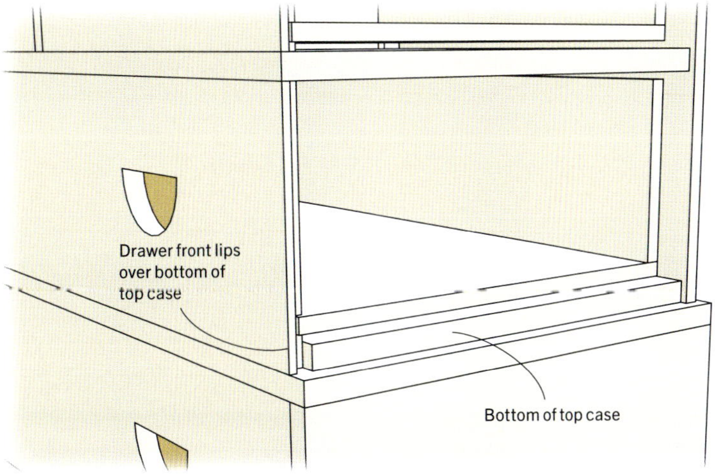

Saw & shoot. Use the ends of the case to mark the finished height of the vertical drawer divider. Then saw and shoot to the line (traditional habits die hard).

Get a grip. Use a cove bit set to make a ½"-deep cut to relieve the inside of the cutout.

Take your time. Using liquid hide glue allows you to take up to 45 minutes to complete the assembly before the glue sets. This makes for easy one-person assembly jobs.

Tape guides the way. I use blue tape to te rarily mark out where my nails should go. I re-roll the tape back on the roll to use it

Drawer parts. Here you can see the rabbets and grooves that make up the drawers. I'm smooth-planing the drawer back before assembly.

First, glue alone. Assemble the drawers with glue and clamps—no nails, screws, or Dominos. The glue alone will hold the parts together for the Domino joinery later.

Drawer detail. Make this bevel with a chisel. The bevel (plus the fact that the drawer back is a bit narrower) makes for a drawer that's easy to operate and insert into the carcase.

Clamp the drawer to your bench with the drawer front facing up. Then lay out and cut the four mortises at each corner. If you own the Domino Support Bracket, which attaches to the underside of the machine, this is the time to use it. The bracket will reduce the chance of the machine tipping down, ruining the joint.

Now paint glue on the Dominos and hammer them into the joints. When the glue dries, cut the Domino flush to the drawer side and plane things smooth.

NOW THE DETAILS

Fit the drawers with a plane. Once they move smoothly, tack some drawer stops in the carcase to keep the drawers in place when closed. I opted to have my drawer fronts 1⁄16" recessed from the front edges of the carcase. This hides small errors and prevents you from having to flush up any irregularities over all the drawer fronts.

The next detail is connecting the top case to the bottom carcase. As mentioned before, this is done with two 1"-diameter dowels that stick up from the bottom carcase that nest into matching holes in the underside of the top carcase. Here's how to make that happen with almost no measuring:

Clamp the top carcase to the bottom carcase so they fit as flush as possible. Now mark on the bottom of the top carcase where you want your dowels to go—about 2" in from the ends and 3" in from the front is fine. Drill a 1⁄16" hole through both carcases at each of these marks. Now unclamp the cases.

You can now use these 1⁄16" holes to guide the tip of your 1"-diameter Forstner bit. Drill 1⁄2"-deep holes in the underside of the top carcase and the top of the bottom carcase. Cut two bits of 1"-diameter oak dowel to about 7⁄8" long. Glue those into the holes in the bottom carcase. If you drilled the pilot holes plumb, then the top case should drop on the bottom case with a nice thunk. If it doesn't, rasp the dowels until things fit nicely.

The last detail before leaving the carcase is to add the brass backplates to the cutouts in the drawer fronts. I used 1⁄16"-thick brass and painted the front black. You can use wood, but I wanted the fingers to find the cool and smooth brass inside the pulls.

I cut the brass to size with a hacksaw and filed the edges smooth—you don't want lacy underwear to catch the corners. Then cut clearance holes and countersinks in the brass—all of this can be done with your woodworking tools set to slow speeds. Screw the brass in place with #8 x 5⁄8" screws.

THE PLINTH

I experimented with several plinths before settling on this simple one. The second-place plinth used 5" rubber casters that were affixed to 3⁄4" x 5" x 5" blocks on the underside of the carcase. It made the whole project easy to move.

Plunge in. The Domino cuts a deep mortise through the drawer side and drawer front.

Paint the Domino. Use plenty of glue. I paint glue in the mortise and on the Domino. Glue is cheap; broken drawer joints are not.

A flush finish. A flush-cut saw makes quick work of removing the extra 2 mm protruding from the drawer sides. A plane finishes the job.

Drawer stops. My drawer stops are 3⁄16"-thick poplar, which was scrap from making the drawers. Tack the stops in place with 1⁄2" brads.

The first-place plinth is also easy to make. It consists of two base pieces that are 1⅜" x 3" x 33". I beveled the ends at 14° then bored 1⅛"-diameter through-holes near the ends for the legs. Then I screwed the two base pieces to the bottom of the carcase.

The legs are 1½" x 1½" x 6½" long octagons. I turned a tenon on the end of each leg to match its mortise, and I made the tenon a tight friction-fit. Then I planed the octagons so they tapered to 1⅜" at the floor.

I wanted the legs to fit tightly so friction would keep the legs in place while the piece was being used. Yet you can remove the legs with a good tug to move the piece. If you want more holding power, consider embedding a rare-earth magnet in the top of each leg and at the bottom of each mortise.

FINISHING

The finish is simple. I used a black aniline dye to color the plinth. Then I sprayed two coats of super-blond shellac on all the parts (sanding lightly between each) and added a coat of beeswax thinned with linseed oil.

The finished piece was intended to be a spec piece that I could sell to help pay my daughter's college tuition. But my wife, Lucy, liked it so much that she claimed it for herself. She doesn't much look like the British Empire's Queen Victoria, but (like Victoria) she gets what she wants.

A hole to pilot you. A 1⁄16" pilot drilled through both carcases makes it easy to drill the 1"-diameter holes for the dowels. (The little block of wood? It's covering the flutes on a countersink bit—the only 1⁄16" bit I have with a hex shaft to fit my right-angle drill.)

Follow the pilot. Put the tip of your Forstner in the pilot hole and drill ½" down. Keep the drill as plumb as possible.

Brass backplate. I considered mortising these into the inside of the drawer front, but that wouldn't have left enough space for your fingers to get into the coved area between the backplate and drawer front.

Plane to taper. Mark the final diameter on the underside of your legs using dividers. Plane down to that line.

Tight fit. Screw the two base pieces of the plinth to the carcase from inside the case. Then fit each leg tightly into its mortise.

SHAKER BLANKET CHEST

This piece from White Water Village shows a Southern influence.

BY MEGAN FITZPATRICK

Store your stuff in style. This blanket chest is based on a 19th-century example from a southwest Ohio Shaker community, but the dovetail layout shows the influence of Southern furniture. In typical fashion, the till lid doubles as a chest lid stay.

Half-blinds galore. I'm usually a tails-first dovetailer. After marking out and cutting the tails, I remove the bulk of the waste with a coping saw. Then, I split the remaining waste in half and chop it out, working toward the middle from both sides until I can't split it any more and the chisel drops into my baseline. (Ideally, I've done a good job with the coping saw so that my first chop is at the baseline.) After transferring the layout to the pin board, I overcut the sockets with the dovetail saw to make waste removal easier in the corners.

Atypical for Shaker blanket chests, this piece (a near replica of an extant example built at Union Village and now at the White Water Shaker Village) has half-blind dovetails on all corners. The layout—side boards with tails at the front, pins at the back—has more in common with a typical sugar chest than with most Shaker blanket chests, which are usually either through-dovetailed or rabbetted and nailed.

So it seems the influence of Southern furniture made it across the Ohio River—at least on this piece.

This chest is a fairly simple build; the bulk of the work is in cutting the 44 half-blind joints on the carcase, after which the 24 through-dovetails for the plinth are a stroll in the park (with the possible exception of cutting the miter on the integral molding). The most difficult step is keeping the three till parts properly aligned while gluing up the carcase (but get a friend to help and it's easy).

I was lucky; I got my hands on several beautiful pieces of wide, 4/4 walnut for the one-board front and back of my chest (I also scored a gorgeous 5/4 piece for the one-board top). But to get the width needed for the ends, I had to glue up panels.

You'll note that I'm not mentioning many exact measurements for my build—and this is one reason I've stated this piece is a "near-replica." The cutlist on page 86 gives the dimensions of the original blanket chest; mine is ever-so-slightly smaller, because after processing the lumber for the carcase, the front board was just shy of the 17³⁄₁₆" width of the original. I wasn't about to go searching for another wide piece; this one was simply too beautiful not to use. And I didn't for even a second consider scabbing on the "missing" ¼", nor did I fret if the thickness of my workpieces was "off" by ¹⁄₁₆".

I suggest you use the same approach for this and most period builds, in the spirit of the original makers. Let the nice wood you have available tell you what size—within reason—the finished project will be, then adjust the dimensions of all your workpieces accordingly instead of slavishly following a cutlist.

START WITH THE CARCASE

The front is a pin board at both ends, the sides have tails at the front corner but pins at the back corner, and the back has tails at both ends. So while the two side pieces are the same length as one another, the front and back differ in length by twice the depth of the pin sockets in my case.

So first, process your carcase pieces using your preferred approach (I turn to machines for the heavy work, then use bench planes to remove the machine marks). Next, lay out and cut the dovetails. Here, I replicated the design on the original, with 11 joints on each corner at a 1:6 slope.

With the carcase joinery complete, dry-fit to make sure the piece goes together square, then knock it apart. Do not get ahead of yourself and rush to glue up; you still need to fit the till. (I don't know about you, but a successful dry-fit makes me want to immediately lunge for the glue bottle; I stuck several notes around my bench and on the front workpiece to remind myself not to.)

TILL WORK

The chest carcase forms the ends and back of the till, so there are but three pieces to cut: the bottom, front, and top. The front is ½" wider than the bottom, and extends past it so they meet flush at the exposed long edges, in effect forming a butt joint between the two (though they are not actually joined). I milled the three pieces to thickness and width, but left them overlong.

After pulling the thickness from the till front and bottom, mark on the interior of the carcase front and back the location and extents of the two dados for the till front and the two grooves for the bottom, then chop them out with a chisel to a depth of about ¼".

Now dry-fit the carcase again and determine the distance between the joints' floors. (I find pinch sticks to be more accurate than trying to read a tape on an interior measurement.)

Cut the bottom and front to that length, minus a hair if you'd like to make the glue-up easier.

But you're not ready to glue up yet—there's still the till lid to go.

That lid edge is molded; you can replicate the original molding as I did (a pattern for both the till and chest lid molding is on page 85; simply scale it down for the till stock), design your own or choose a profile that matches your router bits if you prefer that route. After cutting a series of rabbets and grooves on the table saw for the bulk of the waste removal, then planing chamfers to guide the molding planes, I used No. 2 hollow and round planes to shape the profile for the lid molding.

If your plane irons are sharp and you do a good job of removing all the flats, you shouldn't need to sand much.

After you're satisfied with the look of the molding, cut the lid to the same length as the till front and bottom. Now determine the length it needs to be to fit between the sides yet still swing freely. (I again turned to my pinch sticks for this "measurement.")

To make the integral hinge for the till lid, saw stopped cuts at both ends (start from the molded edge), leaving about ⅜" or so of material at the unmolded edge from which to form round tenons. I marked out and made most of each cut at the table saw, stopping short of the full length to accommodate the blade radius. I finished off the crosscut with a panel saw, then made the short rip cut on each end with a backsaw.

I marked out the round tenons by lightly tapping a ¼" Forstner bit on the end of each, about ⅛" in from the back edge, then used a flush-cut saw to cut the perimeter around the tenon where it meets the lid before trimming the tenon to round with a chisel. (The tenons needn't be perfectly circular.)

With all the till pieces cut, knock the back off your carcase and insert the till bottom and front into their mortises. Set the lid in place atop the till and mark the hole location (you may want a shop helper to hold things in place

Dados & grooves. Mark the locations for the till front and bottom, then knife in the edges. Use a chisel (bevel side toward the waste of course) to deepen your knife lines, then make a series of across-the-grain cuts into the waste. Chisel out the waste and repeat until you reach ¼" depth (or slightly less). You can use a router plane to clean up the bottom if you like—but no one will ever see it.

Pinch sticks. My usual pinch sticks are too long to fit across the chest's depth, so I cobbled together a set with two offcuts, a binder clip and some blue tape, sticky side out (then wrapped with a piece of tape sticky side in to keep things nice and neat).

while you do this). To mark the location on the other side, I set the carcase back in place and marked the round tenon location there as well. (While you could use various measuring devices for all this, I find it more accurate and quicker to work from the actual workpieces.)

Now knock everything apart for the last time and drill ¼" holes for the round tenons—an operation I elected to perform at the drill press so my hole was straight and I could set a depth stop.

Make sure your round tenons fit in their holes. It's OK if they're a little loose; if they're too tight, trim off excess material with a chisel or knife.

As a final check before glue-up, you may want to dry-fit one of the two right carcase corners, insert all the till pieces in their respective mortises, then open the till lid to make sure it will clear the carcase side. If it doesn't swing clear, round over or chamfer the back edge of the till lid until it does.

Make sure you smooth-plane or sand the till parts before moving on—it will be difficult to get a nice surface on these pieces once the carcase is together.

GET THE GLUE

I prefer liquid hide glue (warmed in a soothing, warm-water bath), which gives me about 30–45 minutes of open time and cleans up easily with water. Why? Because just in case things go

FRONT

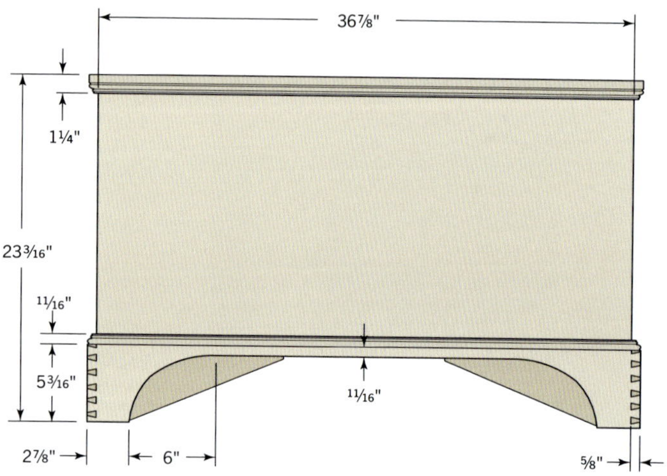

TILL DETAIL

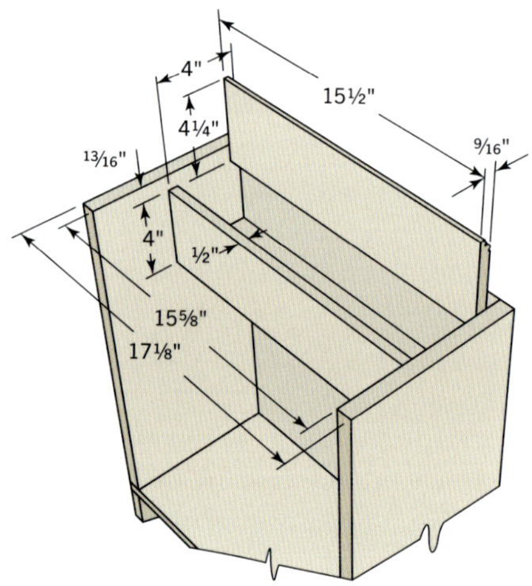

BACK

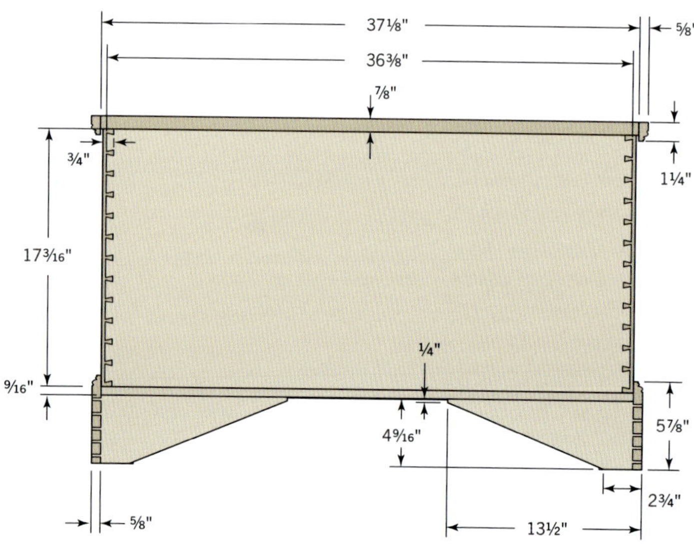

SIDE

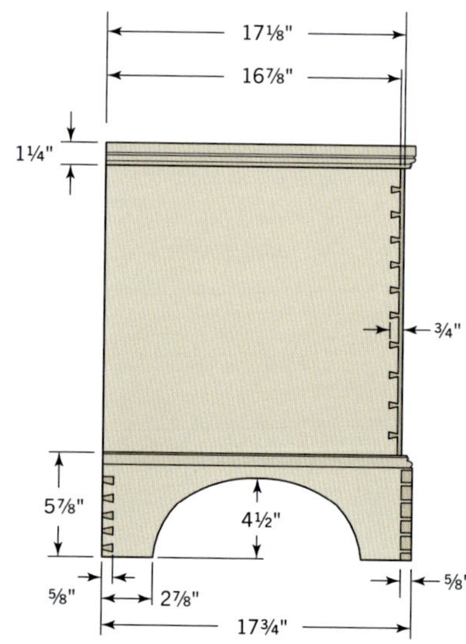

south, the hide glue is reversible with water and heat (also a handy attribute should a repair ever be needed).

Most carcases can be knocked together sans helper, but for this one, a few extra hands are useful to keep the till pieces in their mortises as you seat the dovetails.

Because you've by now done several dry-fits, you've no doubt realized that the dovetail layout dictates the back (a tail board at both ends) goes on last. Smear glue in the front's sockets, seat the two sides, then put the till pieces in place. You can put a bit of glue in the mortises for the till bottom and front to keep things from potentially rattling around, but it's not strictly necessary. Do not, of course, let glue get into the round mortises for the till lid.

Now put glue in the sockets on the back end of the side boards, and knock the back in place while making sure the till parts seat simultaneously in their housings.

Check for square (again, I find pinch sticks easier for this than a tape measure), make any adjustments needed, then clamp it together...or not, if your dovetails all seat perfectly and your carcase is square with no mechanical aids (I hope to someday be that perfect). Now go enjoy a 24-hour break while the glue cures. Or start working on the bottom, plinth, and lid while you wait.

The bottom on the extant Shaker chest is simply one board of 9⁄16"-thick poplar that's nailed on. I couldn't find a piece of poplar that wide, and the original has a split right down the middle, so I decided on a two-board bottom with a tongue-and-groove joint down the middle.

To dress it up a bit, I also cut a bead on the grooved board—which should have gone on the tongue board so as not to weaken the grooved piece, but my 3⁄16" beading plane couldn't seat above the tongue on the thin board. (While I perhaps shouldn't admit my considered fudging, you may run into the same difficulty if you decide on a bead, so...)

Use clout nails to secure the bottom in place, then trim the edges as necessary so that the bottom fits flush to the case sides all around.

Rabbet first. Save yourself a lot of time (and get better results) by cutting rabbets and grooves to remove as much waste as possible before using hollows and rounds to shape a molding profile. I cut these at the table saw.

Molding planes. The rabbets and grooves will help to guide the molding planes as you shape the profile. A light touch is key when using these traditional tools.

LID MOLDING PROFILE

Grid = 1⁄4" squares

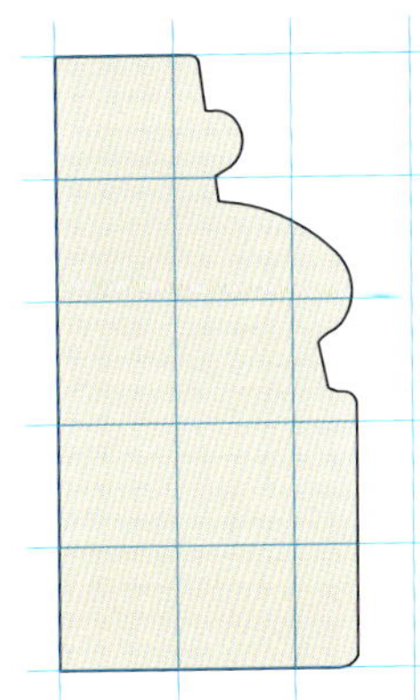

MORE MOLDING WORK

As on the till lid, both the applied lid molding and the integral plinth molding were cut using hollows and rounds. That means finding two straight-grained pieces of stock that are at least 75" in length, and for the plinth, 6" wide. (Note that on the plinth, much of the wood will eventually be cut away, so it's OK if there are knots and such across the width, as long as they're in the waste area.) For the best results on hand-cut molding, you want everything to be from one continuous piece so that the profile flows cleanly from end to end. And when you fit the pieces, you'll want as little waste as possible at the miters (which also holds true for router-cut moldings, though it's more a

Square to round. A flush-cut saw makes neat work of cutting a circle around the tenon base. Work your way around the tenon using a chisel to remove the flats until you have something close to a cylinder.

Obligatory glue-up picture. My carcase was slightly out of square at the top; a long clamp from corner to corner fixed it.

CUT LIST & MATERIALS

	NO.	ITEM	DIMENSIONS (INCHES)			MATERIAL
			T	W	L	
☐	1	Front	3/4	7 3/16	36 7/8	Walnut
☐	1	Back	3/4	7 3/16	6 3/8	Walnut
☐	2	Sides	3/4	7 3/16	16 7/8	Walnut
☐	1	Bottom	9/16	17 1/8	36 7/8	Poplar
☐	1	Chest lid	7/8	17 1/4	37 1/8	Walnut
☐	1	Till bottom	1/2	3 1/2	6 1/8*	Walnut
☐	1	Till front	1/2	4	6 1/8*	Walnut
☐	1	Till lid	1/2	4 1/4	6 1/8*	Walnut
☐	1	Plinth front	5/8	5 7/8	38 1/8	Walnut
☐	2	Plinth sides	5/8	5 7/8	17 3/4	Walnut
☐	2	Plinth backs	5/8	4 9/16	13 1/2	Walnut
☐	1	Lid molding	5/8	1 1/4	80**	Walnut
☐	2	Butt hinges	3/32	1 1/2	2 1/2	Antique brass
☐	1	Half-mortise chest lock		3 1/2	2 1/4	Brass

*Includes 1/4" at both ends **Includes extra for miters

grain-match consideration than one of profile shape with machined pieces).

The molding profile on both of these pieces is the same, and it's the same as that on the till lid, only larger. Again, cut rabbets and grooves both to remove the bulk of the waste and to guide your molding planes, then cut a 45° chamfer on the edges to be rounded over. For these moldings, I used No. 4 and No. 8 hollows and rounds.

Set the lid molding aside when you're done and work on the plinth. On it, you'll cut through-dovetails at all four corners, with a miter joint at the top front corners where the molding meets.

Note that the front of the plinth is a tail board, and the sides get pins at the front and tails at the back. But for now, concentrate on one front corner. Cut the plinth pieces to length, but don't leave much extra for the joinery; again, the pieces should go together with as little waste at the molded edge as possible, so that minor variations from your plane work aren't noticeable.

On the original, there is a half-tail at the bottom and top of the layout, so I replicated that. The top edge of the top tail is a 90° cut—not a 1:6 slope as on the rest—so the tail nestles under the bottom of the molding (see "Fussy fit" at right). Cut the joints and remove the waste, but leave the molded edge at full length until the dovetails are done.

Mark a 45° angle to define the miter angle on each piece (I used a 6" adjustable square and a marking knife, and nicked across the high points on the molding) then cut straight down on the waste side of your line. The closer you get to the finish cut the less remaining work there is to do, but don't get overconfident; better to fuss with the final fit a few times than overcut here and have a resultant gap in your miter.

Knock the joints together as far as they'll go, make sure the boards are 90° to one another, then use a flush-cut saw to cut straight down between the two miters to remove a sliver of material. Knock the joints more tightly together, check the fit, then cut again (and again) as necessary. The saw will bind in the cut—and that's a good thing it means the joint is tight. Adjust right and left with the saw as necessary to bring everything together tightly at 45°.

With the first corner dry-fit, mark the baseline on the other end and repeat.

Refer to the Back illustration on page 84 and note that the front and sides of the plinth are nailed around the carcase; the narrower back pieces sit under the carcase bottom. Cut them to length, and complete the plinth joinery (tails on the back pieces, pins on the sides).

Now knock everything apart, and lay out then cut the curves on the front and sides. Leave the back pieces square until after the plinth is applied; that makes it easier to glue and clamp it in place. The angles are easy to cut afterward with a jigsaw or panel saw.

Glue up the plinth while wrapping it around the carcase (this will help make sure they fit flush to one another). Be gentle while knocking the plinth together; with the curves cut, there is little material remaining so the pieces can easily snap. Nail it in place on the front and sides, and glue the back pieces to the carcase bottom. Add glue blocks at all four corners.

LID, HARDWARE & FINISH

Cut your lid panel to size (about ⅛" wider and longer than the carcase to allow it to easily open and close), and smooth-plane or sand the inside to a finished state; once you apply the molding, it will be darn near impossible to get into the corners.

Rip the lid molding from its motherboard, smooth the saw cut as necessary, then fit and cut the miters. Apply glue to the front piece and a few inches back along each side piece to force movement to the back, then nail the molding in place with cut nails.

I installed a half-mortise lock similar to the one on the original piece—though I'm not sure that lock was installed by the Shakers (it could have been if this chest was in an elder's room; if not, the lock was likely added by a later owner). The hinges are two 2½"-long butt hinges; on the original, the two hinges were each only about 1" long, which seemed too small (though they fit the mortises perfectly, so they were not likely replacements). If you can, use slot screws instead of Phillips screws (if you want period-correct heads). And yes, my screws are all clocked.

The finish is three coats of shop-made oil/varnish blend, rubbed out with 600-grit sandpaper after each of the first two coats was dry.

This near-reproduction is destined for White Water Shaker Village, as a companion to its inspiration.

In the groove. After getting it set up, a Stanley No. 45 combination plane makes quick work of the groove for the tongue-and-grooved bottom.

Fussy fit. Once the dovetail just under the molding is fully seated, stop trimming the miter. It can't close up any more.

TRAVELING TOOLBOX

Bodger and blacksmith Don Weber shows how to effectively combine power and hand-tool techniques to build a simple and sturdy toolbox.

BY DON WEBER

I'm a bodger and a blacksmith, making tables and chairs in iron and wood. When I'm not in the shop, I'm journeying to woodworking shows to demonstrate the spring pole lathe or teach workshops in traditional woodworking and metal smithing. I travel quite a bit, and if you've ever watched the way the baggage handlers deal with your luggage, you'll understand why I built an oak box banded in iron to carry my woodworking tools.

The tool box described here was made of quartersawn oak from a winery in northern California. I've built instrument cases for rare and antique musical instruments, and I've found the lids moved considerably with humidity changes. So with this toolbox I've allowed the top and bottom to float in a groove in the sides and ends, much like a frame-and-panel door.

I had the oak boards resawn to ½" thick. All the joinery was done on a table saw with the help of a rebate plane (here in America we call a "rebate" a "rabbet," but I prefer the traditional English term), a Stanley No. 5 (jack plane) and a low-angle block plane. I reinforced the corners of the box with ⅛"-diameter locust pins because I forged corner brackets (not shown here) as well as the hinges, latch and handles. (I've been influenced by the Tansu hardware of Japanese chests.)

EDGE JOINTING BY HAND

The top and bottom panels were made by gluing up two boards edge-to-edge. I prepare the edge for gluing with my jack plane (Mr. Jack, I call him). Cabinetmakers of old would use a longer jointer plane, but a board of this length can be accurately planed with the shorter jack. Use your fingers as a fence along the face of the board as you plane each edge. Check your results with a try square.

If you've done a good job with the plane, you should be able to create what we call a "rubbed" joint. This is where you glue each edge and rub the mating edges together until the glue begins to set up. A clamp or two is a good idea while the glue cures.

REBATES BY HAND & POWER

I cut the rebates on the side pieces by first defining the joint's shoulder with my table saw and then reducing the thickness of the tongue with my rebate plane, a vintage Record No. 778. Set the height of the table saw's blade to half

Joint the edges. I use my jack plane to joint the edges of the side boards. The plane's iron is slightly cambered across its width to allow me to correct an out-of-square edge.

Glue up. When gluing up a panel, I rub the glue joint up and down to ensure a gap-free joint.

Clamp it. A couple of clamps across the joint are good insurance—even if you have a good edge joint. The cauls keep the panel flat.

Angle. Start the plane at an angle as shown. After each pass bring the tool a bit more level. This makes a square joint.

Chamfer. Chamfering the edges of the top and the raised panel with a block plane softens the look.

the thickness of the stock of the sides and ends, which is ⅜" in this case. Set the rip fence so your rebate will be ¾" wide. Cut the shoulder on the ends of the sides. Reduce the thickness of the joint with your rebate plane as shown bottom left.

For those purists out there, you can cut the rebate entirely with a rebate plane (or a Stanley No. 10, a carriage-maker's bench plane). Just be sure to use the plane's side nickers to score across the grain to prevent your grain from tearing out as you cut the joint.

The edges of the top and bottom panel were rebated all around in the same manner to fit in the groove cut in the sides and ends of the box. I set the raised portion of the panels so they are flush with the top and bottom edges of the sides. Note that the rebates on the ends of the panel are ⅜" wide. The rebate on the long edges is a different width, ¼". This arrangement allows the panel to expand across its width but not along its length. And that is proper cabinetmaking.

A small chamfer is planed around the inner sides of the box frame, and the raised portion of the top and bottom to create a visual break when the panel moves with humidity variation.

PLOWING THE GROOVES

The top and bottom panels are fit into the grooves in the sides and ends. You could cut this groove using your table saw. But if you have a plow plane, this is the place to put it to use.

The plow plane is designed to cut grooves of different widths, which are varied by changing the cutter in the tool. The location of the groove is determined by the tool's fence, which bears against the edge of the work during the cut. The depth of the groove is determined by the tool's depth stop. Once the joint reaches its final depth, the tool will then cease to cut.

GLUE, DRILL & PEG

Glue and clamp the ends to the sides with the top and bottom panels in place. Be careful not to get glue in the groove or the panel can't expand and contract as it needs. When the glue has cured, drill ⅛"-diameter holes in the corner joints to accept the ⅛" locust pins.

The top is cut away from the glued-up box 1½" from the top edge, using a table saw. After the first two cuts are made, wedges are inserted in the slots to keep the saw blade from binding. A few pieces of masking tape keep the wedges in place.

With the saw cut complete, clean up the tooling marks on the top and bottom using a plane, scraper, or (my favorite) a small scraping plane.

The hardware for my box was hand forged in my blacksmith's shop, though there is some decent hand-wrought

HAND-FORGED HARDWARE

I hand-forged the hardware you see here in my blacksmith shop. You could find a local blacksmithing workshop or purchase reproduction hardware for your toolbox (see Tools and Supplies listings on p. 149).

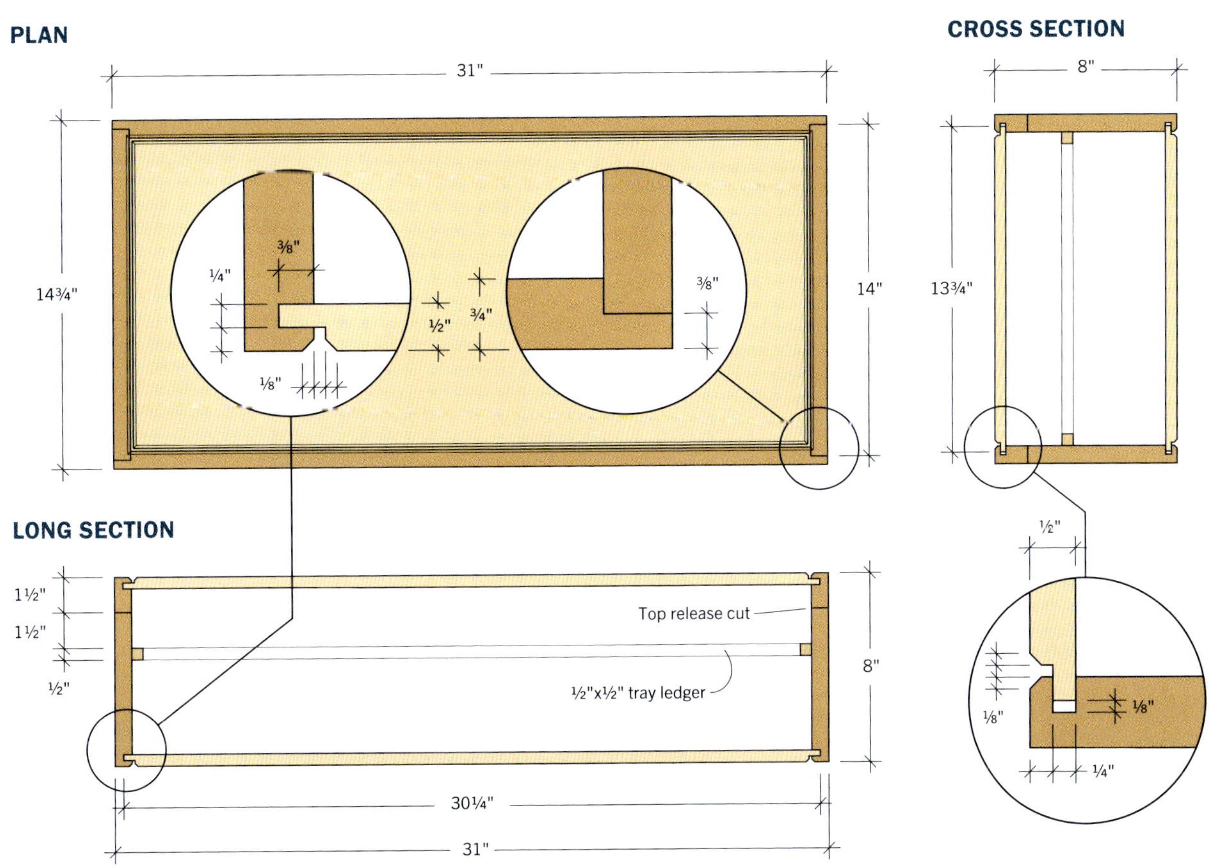

hardware out there. To fasten the handles to the box, I added a ½" x ½" ledger to the inside of the box to strengthen the attachment of the handles as well as to provide a ledge for a tray for small tools.

All surfaces were dressed with a cabinet scraper and finished with an oil varnish (one pint marine spar varnish, one pint boiled linseed oil, and enough gum turpentine to thin to the consistency of half-and-half).

Once rubbed up with a Scotch-Brite pad and some Briwax, the job is done. I have done a lot of traveling with this toolbox, inevitably filling it with more tools than it should carry, and it is still doing its job admirably.

Bore holes. Here I'm using a hand drill (sometimes called an eggbeater drill) to bore the pilot holes for my locust pins.

CUT LIST & MATERIALS

	NO.	ITEM	DIMENSIONS (INCHES) T	W	L	MATERIAL
☐	1	Top	½	13¾	30¼	Oak
☐	1	Bottom	½	13¾	30¼	Oak
☐	2	Ends	¾	8	14	Oak
☐	2	Sides	¾	8	31	Oak
☐	2	Hinges				
☐	2	Handles				
☐		Pins	⅛-dia.			Locust

Make the lid. Carefully part the lid on the table saw with wedges to hold the kerf open (left). Once the lid has been parted from the bottom, plane or scrape the sawn edges of the toolbox to remove the tooling marks (right).

GREENE & GREENE-STYLE BLANKET CHEST

A simple approach to a sublime design.

BY MARC SPAGNUOLO

I've been enamored of Greene & Greene furniture since my early days of woodworking, well before I possessed the skills to produce such a piece. Since that time, this style has become a regular part of my woodworking vocabulary, and I enjoy making reproductions and interpretations of classic Greene & Greene designs. This blanket chest is a re-imagining of an original piece designed by the Greene brothers (Charles and Henry) for the Thorsen House in Berkeley, Calif.

My wood of choice for this project was khaya, sometimes referred to as African mahogany. The original Thorsen House box was made from red oak—so don't hesitate to use a domestic species if exotic woods don't suit your taste or budget.

The bottom of the blanket chest is made from ¾" plywood, and you can save a bunch of cash by using a domestic-veneered species instead of seeking out mahogany-faced stock. The ebony trim comes from a 2" x 2" x 12" turning blank, which should provide enough ebony for several projects.

The case panels are glued up from several narrower boards. Take care to

SECTION

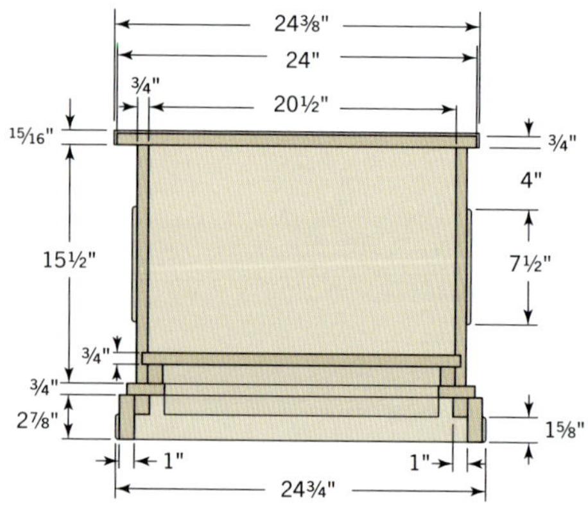

FRONT

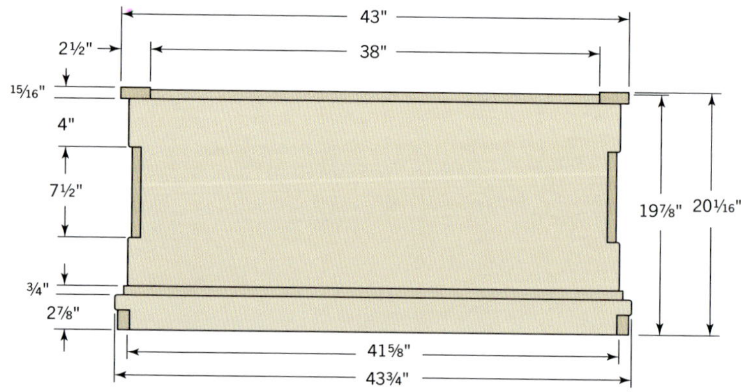

arrange your boards in such a way that they complement one another in both grain pattern and color. After cutting to length and width, the wide finger joints are milled on each end with a router and a template.

SIMPLE TEMPLATE

Technically you need two templates: one for the female part of the joint and one for the male. Here's a cool way to make them both in one shot. Cut a piece of ½" or ¾" sheet-good stock to approximately 16" x 24", making sure the corners are perfectly square. Rip the piece into two 4"-wide strips and one 7½"-wide strip. With the 7½" strip in the center, glue the three pieces back together after sliding the center strip out exactly 11⁄16". Just like that, you have a two-in-one template that matches the 15½" width of our case panels.

The protruding fingers of the case joints have 3⁄16" roundovers. Save yourself some work later by including them in the template. I use a no-frills method for making them; use a ⅜" drill bit as a layout guide, then use a sanding block to create the actual profile.

Trace the shape of the finger joints on each chest side, then cut away the excess material. Stay at least 1⁄16" off the line. With the template clamped to the workpiece, a router outfitted with a bearing-guided pattern bit creates the finger joints on both ends of each board.

The inside corners need to be squared, then you can dry-fit the case and evaluate each joint individually. In all likelihood, the finger joints will be just a bit too tight. Use a chisel and light paring strokes to allow the fingers to nest into one another with ease.

The bottom panel of the chest rests in a groove that runs around the inside of the case. The groove is cut using a router outfitted with an edge guide and an undersized plywood bit. (Most ¾" plywood is never truly ¾" thick, so I use

Slide it. Moving the center piece of the template and reassembling it produces mating profiles on each end of the template.

Cut close. Saw close to the pattern lines, then use a bearing-guided bit in the router to create joints that match the template.

Down below. The single fingers on the base can be cut at the table saw.

a plywood bit specifically designed for this purpose that's 1⁄32" undersized.)

The 3⁄8"-deep groove on the side panels runs from one end to the other. But on the front and back panels, a through-groove would be visible from the outside of the case. Those grooves have to stop before the end of the panel. The router bit leaves a rounded shape at the end of the groove; use a chisel to square it up.

The base for the chest consists of a deck, a finger-jointed base and 1" x 1¼" cleats installed for additional support.

The deck is a large mitered frame. The 45° miters are cut at the miter saw using a stop-block for repeatability. To reinforce the miters, I installed a small loose tenon at each joint. Biscuits, dowels, or pocket screws would work, too. Once the glue dries, I use a No. 80 cabinet scraper to smooth the frame and level the joints.

The base parts are milled from 5/4 stock and have finger joints at each end. There's no need for a template here. Simply measure and mark out the joinery, then cut to the lines. It's a good idea to test-fit the base parts as you go to ensure they fit together perfectly.

I'VE GOT A SECRET (DRAWER)

As designed, the base structure has a lot of dead space. The optional hidden drawer provides an opportunity to recover that space in a very cool way. The base side becomes the drawer front and a frame structure supports the drawer box. You can make the drawer as large or small as you want. Just make sure you leave room for the cleats used to attach the base to the deck.

Build the drawer and frame, double-checking the measurements against your actual workpieces. This drawer doesn't require the level of precision we usually aspire to, so I err on the side of caution by giving the drawer some extra clearance. Unlike regular

EXPLODED VIEW

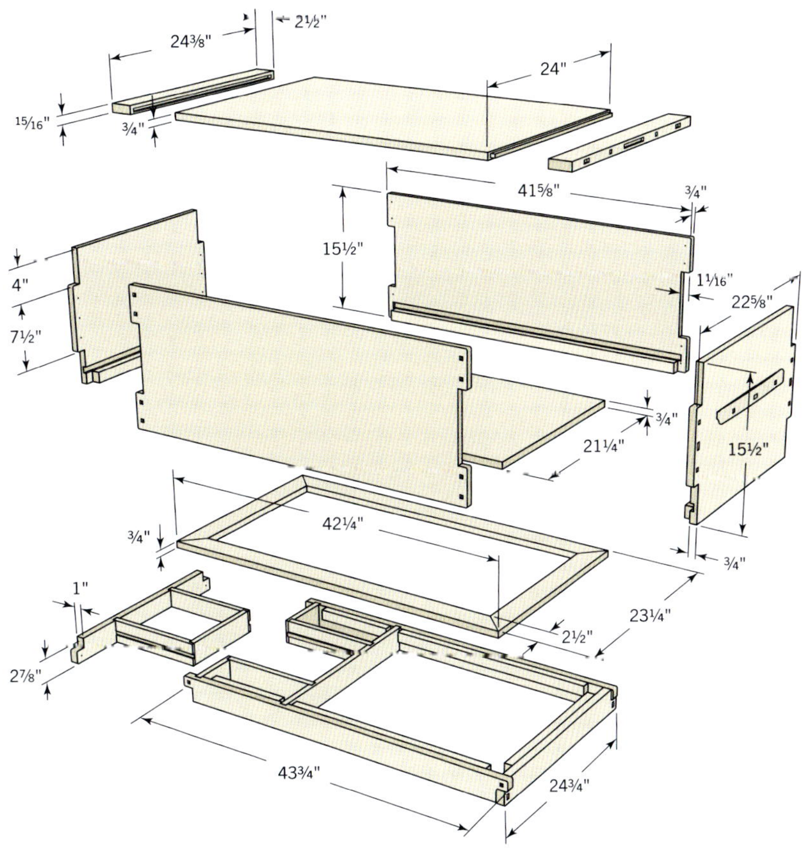

Under the end. The drawer should slide easily and the drawer front should nest snugly below the base front and back.

Two steps. Mortises for the ebony plugs are created by punching a square hole, then removing the waste with a drill.

This, not that. Mark the edges to be rounded over with chalk to help prevent shaping the wrong edges.

Simple assembly. Screws located under the ebony plugs hold the case together.

Second time around. Another set of cleats help hold the base firmly to the deck and case.

drawers, this one is at the bottom of a heavy case and it won't be convenient to adjust should it ever bind.

The drawer parts attach to the base side (the drawer front) with sliding-dovetail joints, and the bottom slips into grooves cut in all four parts. The frame pieces are cut to size and fit in dado joints at the base front and back.

The drawer runners are glued into grooves cut in the sides of the drawer compartment. The drawer receives a slightly wider and deeper groove to allow about 1⁄32" extra play as it slides in and out. The key is to cut the grooves the same distance from the top of each piece (1⅜"). This will keep the drawer flush with the top of the framework and prevent binding.

The base is assembled with glue and screws. Once dry, test-fit the drawer. If the drawer binds at all, put on your investigative cap and determine the source, then use a chisel or scraper to relieve the offending material.

BEHIND THE PLUGS

The blanket chest is held together primarily with screws. Ebony plugs not only hide the screw heads, they also give the piece that classic Greene & Greene styling. The mortises for the ebony plugs need to be cut prior to assembly. Lay out the mortises as shown in the drawing (pp. 94 and 95).

I like to draw each square mortise using a plastic square template. While this may seem like overkill, it actually serves as a sanity check that helps me avoid misplaced plugs. The mortises are then cut into the case and base parts using a ⅜" square hole punch.

The chest has ⅛" roundovers on all the long edges of the case and 3⁄16" roundovers on the breadboard ends and base. A router can do the bulk of the work but some areas need to be hit with a rasp and sandpaper to complete the profile.

THE PARTS BECOME ONE

With the blanket chest case dry-assembled, measure and cut the ¾"-thick plywood bottom panel to size. The panel can then be glued into the groove on the case front and the rest of the case pieces will come together easily. Using glue on the wide finger joints is optional because the unit is held together with screws. Clamps hold the assembly together as you drive screws. Be sure to check the case for square. Use a diagonal clamp to make any necessary corrections.

Attaching the deck and base to the assembled case is easiest to do with the case upside down. A set of cleats are glued to the case then flushed to the bottom edge. The cleats provide extra support, as well as a safe zone for driving screws. The deck is then centered on the case, and screwed into position through countersunk holes.

Before permanently attaching the base to the deck, it's a good idea to drill, countersink, then screw and glue the cleats to the base. Trying to do this work later proves difficult. With the cleats attached, the base is then centered on the deck and attached with #8 x 1¾" screws.

ON TOP OF IT ALL

The blanket chest lid has breadboard ends that stabilize the lid panel and add depth and interest. The breadboards are joined to the panel with a long tongue-and-groove joint. The groove is cut into the breadboards using a drop cut at the router table; make sure to stop prior to the blowing out the ends. The tongue, with its end notched to fit the groove, is routed on the lid panel. Look for a snug fit.

The ends are then screwed into the lid panel through several mortises created for the ebony bars and plugs. The long center bar isn't functional, but it certainly wins style points. The ⅜" x ⅜" mortises are made using the ⅜" square punch. The long mortises are cut at the router table; be careful to drop and lift the workpiece using layout lines as a guide. The router bit leaves a rounded corner so use a chisel to chop the ends square.

The breadboards are then drilled with a 3⁄16" drill bit. The holes are oversized to allow for wood movement as the lid panel expands and contracts.

Round over the edges of the breadboards and the lid panel before assembly. Attach the breadboard ends to the panel using a bit of glue at the center, then drive 3"-long screws into the holes to keep the ends tight to the top.

SCULPTED HANDLE

The handles may look simple at first glance, but the arch-and-cove profiles present a few challenges. Before shaping the handles, cut the mortises for the ebony plugs.

CUT LIST & MATERIALS

	NO.	ITEM	DIMENSIONS (INCHES) T	W	L	MATERIAL	
CHEST							
☐	2	Case front & back	¾	15½	41⅝	Khaya	
☐	2	Case ends	¾	15½	22⅝	Khaya	
☐	1	Case bottom	¾	21¼	40¼	Plywood	
☐	2	Deck front/back	¾	2½	42¼	Khaya	
☐	2	Deck ends	¾	2½	23¼	Khaya	
☐	2	Base front & back	1	2⅞	43¾	Khaya	
☐	2	Base ends	1	2⅞	24¾	Khaya	Optional drawer front
☐	2	Handles	⅞	1⅜	14⅜	Khaya	
☐	1	Lid panel	¾	24	39	Khaya	½ TBE*
☐	2	Breadboard ends	15⁄16	2½	24⅜	Khaya	
☐	1	Plug material	2	2	12	Ebony	
SUPPLIES							
☐	4	Rare-earth magnets	⅛	½-dia.			
☐	4	60 in.-lb. torsion hinges				Rustic bronze	
OPTIONAL DRAWER							
☐	2	Drawer sides	¾	2¾	12½	Khaya	
☐	1	Drawer back	¾	2¾	10⅛	Khaya	
☐	1	Drawer bottom	¾	9⅞	11⅞	Poplar	
☐	1	Frame cross brace	¾	2⅞	23	Khaya	
☐	2	Frame sides	¾	2⅞	12¼	Khaya	
☐	2	Drawer runners	½	½	11⅞	Khaya	
☐	2	Frame returns	¾	2⅞	6	Khaya	

*TBE = Tongue Both Ends

On the end. The groove in the breadboard end fits over the tongue of the top panel. Screws in oversized holes hold the two pieces together.

Undercover. Ebony plugs will cover the screw heads after the breadboard ends are attached.

Back up. Scrap wood behind the handle blank makes it easier to control the work as the cove is routed in the end.

Double duty. The curved template is used as a router fence that supports the arched handle while the cove profile is routed.

Hold up. A block of MDF supports the handle as it is screwed in place to ensure that the handle is positioned accurately.

To shape the arched top of the handle, I use a curved template to help trace the shape of the arch, and to later serve as a router fence. Start with a piece of ¾"-thick sheet stock cut to approximately 10" x 32" (sized for clamping on a router table).

Mark the center point, then measure out 10" in each direction. Mark the peak of the arch 5⁄16" up on the centerline. Draw the curve from the peak to the 10" marks using a drawing bow. If you don't have a drawing bow, draw the same layout 1" in from the edge and use nails to hold a bending strip in position. Cut the curve with a jigsaw or bandsaw and smooth the arc using a spindle sander, rasps, or a flexible sanding strip.

With the curve established, transfer the arc to the top of each handle. Align the center of the curve with the center of the handle stock and each end with lines drawn 3⁄16" down, leaving 11⁄16". Trim to your lines. I use a stationary belt sander to remove the stock to create the arch, but spokeshaves and rasps are other options.

At the router table, I use a ⅝" roundnose or core-box router bit to make the cove that goes around the perimeter of the handle. I start with the ends, using a backer board for additional support.

The long sides are routed using the curved template as a fence. Note that the workpiece is pushed from left to right (instead of right to left like you normally do) because the workpiece is behind the bit. (This process is a little tricky, so exercise caution and make the profile cut with multiple passes.)

Round over the handle and sand it thoroughly to make sure there are no sharp corners, except at the base where the handle attaches to the case.

The handles are glued and screwed to the case sides 8¾" up from the deck. I use scrap to support the handle while I drill and drive the 1⅛"-long screws. Double-check your screw length to ensure they won't punch through the interior of the case.

A PASSEL OF PLUGS

The blank of ebony is cut into sticks that are 1⁄64" over ⅜" square. The blanks are first cut into wide strips, which are then laid flat and cut into sticks. Because cutting thin strips can be dangerous, use a sacrificial push block.

To pillow the ebony plugs, I use a method I learned from William Ng. It involves a drill, a variety of sandpaper grits, and a soft foam pad. With a chisel, chamfer the corners of the last inch of each stick. This allows the stick to fit into a standard ⅜" drill chuck.

Starting with 80 grit, pulse the drill with the end grain of the stick resting on the sandpaper and let the weight of the drill do the work. The sandpaper can be backed up with anything that has give. Move from one grit to the next until you reach 1,000 grit to bring the surface to a polished shine.

With the pillow created on the end of the stick, a simple jig is used to cut the plug off the end. My jig is made from scrap and holds the stick snug for sawing, guides the saw blade for a nice square cut, and ensures each plug is the same length.

The remaining ebony sticks can be further trimmed at the table saw for use as bars, ripping them down to about ¼" in one dimension and leaving the other dimension at 1⁄64" over ⅜". To create the pillowed effect on the bars, I use a ½"-radius roundover bit and lower the bit so that it just catches the vertical portion of the cutter. With the help of another jig (p. 99, bottom left), you can safely take two passes to create the pillowed effect.

The square plugs are tapered on each side so they wedge into the mortises. This is done with a few strokes of a chisel. For the bars, I use sandpaper to create the taper. To install the plugs and bars, use glue and a plastic-headed hammer. The key is to use light but firm taps that leave the plugs proud of the surface. Be careful not to push the plug in too far because it is very difficult to remove without doing damage.

Spin it. A series of sandpaper grits is lined up on a flexible pad, and the drill spins the ebony into each grit.

All the same. This jig is used to cut each plug to an identical length.

DYE & LACQUER

When it comes to Greene & Greene projects, it's hard to argue with the beauty and elegance provided by the right stain. The dye mixture I use is a 1:2 ratio of General Finishes Medium Brown to Orange. The dye is water-based, so I raise the grain with water and sand before applying the dye. The dye is spray-coated liberally, then I wipe away any standing liquid with a pre-moistened terry cloth sponge.

For a topcoat I used three coats of CAB acrylic lacquer with light sanding between each coat. After a week of cure time, I rubbed the surface with a 2,000-grit abrasive pad. The high grit doesn't change the sheen of the finish, but it produces a glass-smooth surface.

Before calling this project complete, there are a few loose ends to tie up, including the drawer magnets, the hinges, and corner blocks (to raise the chest off the floor).

The hidden drawer is held closed with rare-earth magnets. I used them on the inside of the drawer face, but outside the drawer box. The ½"-diameter magnets are epoxied in shallow holes.

You can use traditional butt hinges to attach the lid to the case, but I prefer to use torsion hinges. They install in seconds with no mortising and allow the lid to stay open without the need for additional safety mechanisms.

Four corner blocks are cut from scrap wood and attached to the inside corners of the base, with the blocks sitting under the deck. These keep the chest off the ground while allowing the drawer to operate properly. If you have carpet, you may consider longer blocks that raise the case even higher.

This blanket chest serves as a great starting point for anyone looking to dive into the world of Greene & Greene, and it only scratches the surface of what the style has to offer. Even if you're not a fan of Greene & Greene, you probably have an appreciation for the care and attention that goes into creating the eye-catching details.

Hands back. This simple made-from-scrap jig holds the ebony bar so the profile can be safely routed.

A pattern emerges. The dark plugs and bars add a decorative element and hide the screws.

Swing & hold. Torsion hinges serve to hold the lid open without any additional support.

3 | CABINETS

IF YOU'VE HAD ENOUGH OF LIDS, get ready for doors! These mostly wall-hung cabinets are perfect for curios, toiletries, hardware, spices, or whatever else you can think up. Whether you need a passel of drawers, a column of shelves, or just a small cupboard, there's a project here for you. Highlight a beautifully grained door panel, go the more affordable route with a painted finish, or mount a mirror. And don't forget the astonishing variety of hinges available—from European to piano to butt hinges, there is a design to fit your particular project that will also give it some flair.

SHAKER WALL CUPBOARD

A classic form from the New Lebanon Shaker community is easy to build in a few hours.

BY CHRISTOPHER SCHWARZ

Simply red. The original cabinet is cherry with a varnish finish. It looks good in a variety of woods, including this poplar version with a red wash.

If you don't like nails, then perhaps you should turn the page. This small wall cupboard from the New Lebanon Shaker community bristles with them.

The carcase and stiles are nailed together with cut brads. The back is attached with clout nails. And the door is held flat with battens that are secured by clenched nails. I think the nails add to the piece, and, because there are so many different kinds, this project is an excellent introduction to 19th-century cut nails.

QUICK JOINERY—QUICK RESULTS

I've built quite a few of these cabinets in the last couple years because they are an excellent way to teach someone traditional joinery and they can be made quickly (my father received one from me that I banged out in a day).

Begin with the carcase. The carcase sides are the only pieces that have real joinery. Cut 3⁄8"-wide by 3⁄16"-deep rabbets in the bottom edges of the sides. These receive the interior bottom piece. Cut 3⁄8"-wide by 3⁄16"-deep dados for the shelf.

Glue and nail the sides, bottom, and shelf together. I used 2d cut headless brads that I set 1⁄32" below the surface.

True up all the edges of the assembled carcase, then fit the two stiles on the front. They hold the carcase square. Glue and nail these in place with 2d cut headless brads and set those.

The thin top and bottom pieces are each attached in an unusual way. First, round over the front edge and ends of each piece. The thin bottom is merely glued on to the carcase. Note that the bottom extends 1⁄4" beyond the back of the carcase, which creates a rabbet for the back. The top is glued and nailed to the stiles and carcase sides (don't worry—it's the back of the cupboard that handles all the weight).

Now deal with the back. Cut the ogee shapes on the top of the back piece.

Get your bottom on. The thin exterior bottom piece is glued on. Clamp the assembly to your benchtop to help distribute the clamping forces.

Connect the dots. Drill a 1⁄4" hole for the top of the slot and a 3⁄8" hole at the bottom. Connect the holes with a coping saw.

Clenching is a cinch. Drive the tips of your headless brads back into the battens while the door rests on a metal surface.

Then cut the slot that allows you to hang this cupboard on a peg or nail. Here's how. Drill a ¼" hole at the top of the slot. Drill a ⅜" hole at the bottom. Connect the two slots using a coping saw. Attach the back to the carcase using 2d clout nails (no glue).

KEEP YOUR DOOR FLAT

The door is a flat panel of wood. If you don't apply some cross-grain battens to the back, it will warp in short order.

So fit the door in its opening and cut the mortises for your hinges. With the door moving freely, remove it from the cupboard and drill pilot holes through the door and battens for nails

You will clench these nails, which means you'll bend them over on the inside of the door. I used 2d cut headless brads. Drive them through the front of the door and through each batten.

When all the nails are driven in, turn the assembled door over onto a metal surface and hammer the tips of the nails. This will bend them over into the wood, securing them. Then cut the hinge gains, hang the door, and make a turn to hold the door closed. The original also had a little knob, which is best turned on a lathe.

While the finished cabinet will have too much metal to pass through airport security, I guarantee the nails will help your piece last as long as the original.

PROFILE

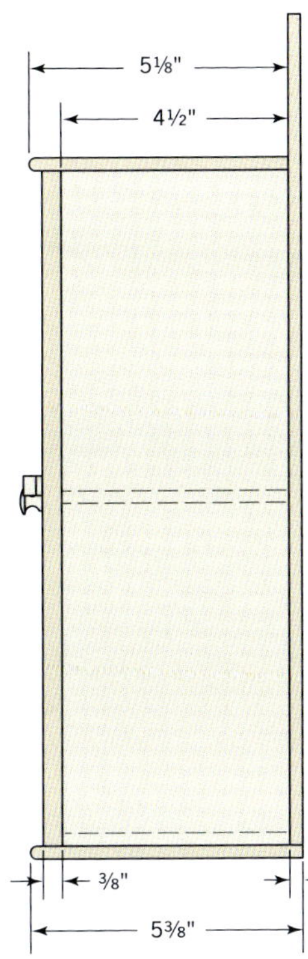

ELEVATION

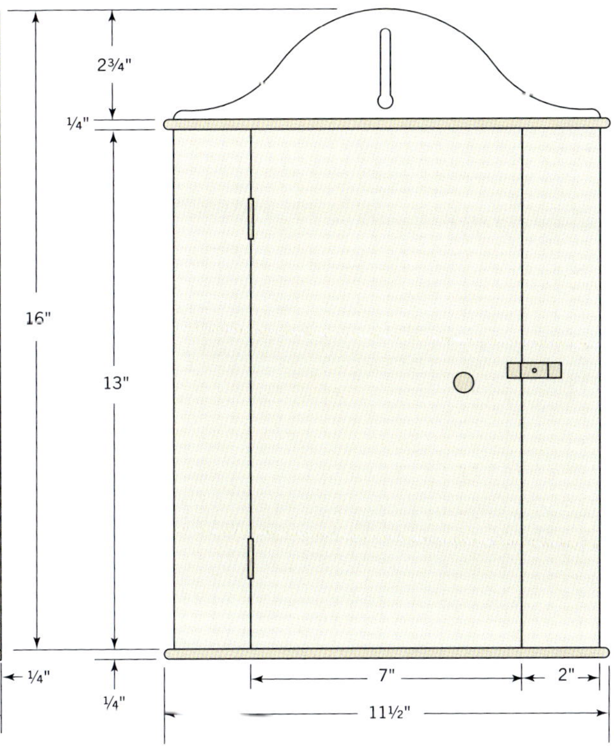

CUT LIST & MATERIALS

	NO.	ITEM	DIMENSIONS (INCHES)			MATERIAL
			T	W	L	
☐	2	Carcase sides	⅜	4½	13	Poplar
☐	2	Stiles	⅜	2	13	Poplar
☐	2	Shelf & sides	⅜	4½	10⅝	Poplar
☐	1	Top	¼	5⅛	11½	Poplar
☐	1	Exterior bottom	¼	5⅜	11½	Poplar
☐	1	Back	¼	11	16	Poplar
☐	1	Door	⅜	7	13	Poplar
☐	2	Battens	⅜	1½	6⅞	Poplar
☐	2	Hinges			1	Brass
☐	1	Knob	½–dia.		½	Poplar
☐	1	Turn	½	½	1½	Poplar

SLOT DETAIL

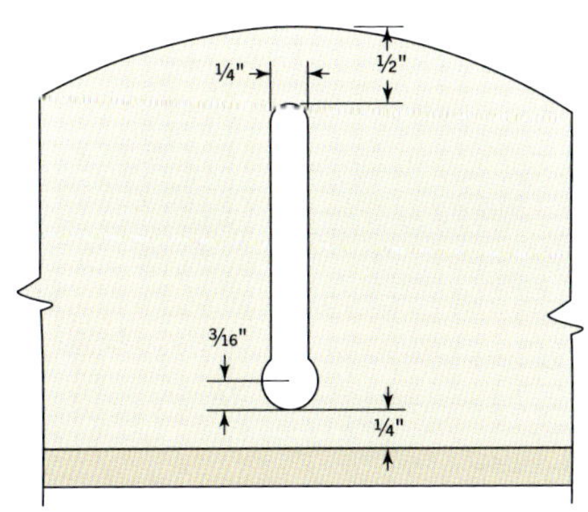

On the set. Roy Underhill's nail cabinet is a converted crate. The cabinet has seen a lot of use and has held up pretty well.

ROY UNDERHILL'S NAIL CABINET

It's a crate. It's a cabinet. It's useful shop furniture.

BY CHRISTOPHER SCHWARZ

One of the enduring features of Roy Underhill's *The Woodwright's Shop* PBS television show is the familiar and rambling backdrop of former projects, parts, tools, and wood that frames most episodes. My favorite item in his shop is his nail cabinet—a pine wall-hung cabinet tucked in the far back corner.

On the inside of the door of the cabinet, Roy has hung a print of a lovely lady holding a bock beer alongside an admiring goat. And while that's some nice lens candy for the television cameras, I'm more attracted to the 21 drawers on the right side of the cabinet. These drawers are more useful to the married woodworker.

Nail cabinets show up frequently in traditional workshops of many trades, and they are illustrated and discussed in books about traditional shops. These cabinets stored the screws, nails, and bolts that a workshop might need. And because these fasteners were valuable, many of the cabinets would have a lock.

The last time I visited Roy, I asked permission to measure and reproduce his nail cabinet, which he purchased from a yard sale in Washington, D.C. As I measured the piece, I was bemused by its unusual construction—it was a finger-jointed carcase covered in nailed-on battens.

Then Roy showed me the reason for the odd construction: The cabinet was built from an old crate for Ohio Blue Tip Matches made by the Ohio Match Co. of Wadsworth, Ohio (1895–1987). For me, this made the project even more fun: I had to first build a crate and then turn it into a wall cabinet.

As a result, some of the construction techniques might seem a bit odd. If you don't like them, feel free to change them. My goal was to make a respectable reproduction of this charming cabinet because I've always liked the one on Roy's show.

Gang-cut tails. Whenever possible, I gang-cut my tail boards, which saves time and (in my opinion) makes it easier to keep the saw 90° to the face of the board. A shallow rabbet on each tail board makes it easy to keep things square during transfer.

As square as possible. Take extra pains to get the carcase square at glue-up. It will save you frustration later when you fit the door and the 21 drawers.

Hide the gap. The shiplapped joints on the long edges of the backboards hide any gap that would open up when the boards shrink in the dry season.

Nails, no glue. Nails will bend, allowing the back to expand and contract without splitting the backboards. Be sure to use nails with a pronounced head to hold the backboards in place.

CONSTRUCTION OVERVIEW

The original is made entirely of pine—probably Eastern white pine—though any dry softwood will do. The carcase of the original crate is joined at the corners with finger joints (though I opted for dovetails on my version). The back of the carcase is nailed-on ⅜"-thick boards that are shiplapped.

The assembled carcase is covered with narrow 1x battens to make the "crate" easy to grab and lift. These battens conceal the joinery on the corners of the carcase.

Once you have your "crate" built, you can turn it into a cabinet. The interior is divided into 21 spaces using thin pieces of pine that are joined with an egg-crate joint. The drawers are simply glued and nailed together; the only thing difficult about the drawers is that you have to build 21 of them.

Finally, the entire cabinet is fronted by a door with mitered corners. The panel of the original door was simply nailed to the inside of the mitered door frame. The panel had cracked over time, so I chose to make my panel float in grooves plowed into the rails and stiles.

The whole thing is finished with shellac and hung on the wall with a French cleat.

More gang-cutting. Lay out the slots on one board, clamp all the dividers together, and make the cut in one go. Here on the table saw, I'm using the saw's miter gauge and a high fence to push the dividers through the blade.

Friction & pins. You should have to knock the joints together with a mallet. Then pin all the intersections with 1"-long headless brads. You'll have to nail them in diagonally to secure them.

Nailing jig. This scrap-wood jig helps you locate exactly where the horizontal dividers are located. It is made using two thin pieces of scrap that are nailed to a scrap of ½"-thick pine. Slip the jig onto the carcase and press one of the thin slips against the dividers inside the case. Trace its location on the exterior. Repeat.

THE WALLS OF THE CRATE

As mentioned above, the walls of the original crate were joined at the corners by narrow finger joints (you can see the joints from the inside where they have separated a bit). I don't have the jigs or desire to make narrow finger joints here, and cutting this machine joint by hand is just silly.

So I joined the case sides, top, and bottom using through-dovetails. The joinery is all covered by battens in the end, so the end result looks the same as the original. For strength, I put the tails on the case sides; the pins are on the top and bottom bits.

Glue up the carcase, paying close attention to keeping the corners square at both the front and rear of the case. I use hide glue for joints like this because it's reversible.

If you can't get the case perfectly square at glue-up, you have one more chance to pull it square with the backboards. The backboards are ⅜"-thick boards of pine that are shiplapped on their long edges and nailed to the back of the case.

I used 3d cut fine finish standard nails to affix the back, though 4d will do.

If your case is out of square, pull the case square with a clamp diagonally across two corners, then nail the backboards in place. This usually helps if the case isn't too racked.

THE INTERIOR DIVIDERS

The interior drawer dividers of the original nail cabinet were obviously built up using miscellaneous scraps that were nailed and glued on to get the job done. Some parts were rough-sawn; some were different species.

Instead of replicating every odd scrap in the cabinet, I simplified the construction while still maintaining its look and function. On the original, the horizontal and vertical dividers are joined with egg-crate joints, and so I used that same joint for my dividers.

The dividers are all ⅜" thick and 6" wide. Every divider has ⅜"-wide slots cut into it. The slots on the horizontal dividers are 2⅞" long. The slots on the vertical dividers are 3" long. When the dividers are knocked together, they will be offset by ⅛" at the front, just like the original.

Lay out the locations of all the slots using the drawings as a guide. I used dividers to step off the drawer sizes, and I used an actual piece of the drawer

Affix the dividers. With the lines drawn on the carcase sides, drive in the cut headless brads and set them 1⁄16" below the surface.

divider to lay out the width of the slots. Note that the three bottom drawers are taller than the others.

I cut the slots on a table saw, though they are easy to cut by hand or on a bandsaw. After cutting the slots, knock the dividers together and pin the joints by toenailing them with headless brads.

With the dividers together, knock the assembly into the carcase. The front edge of the horizontal dividers should be located 1½" from the front edge of the carcase. That spacing allows room for the bin pulls and knobs on the drawers.

The next step is to nail the horizontal dividers to the carcase. This is done easily with a simple jig that makes it (almost) impossible to miss with your nails. (See the bottom photo on p. 110 for details on the jig.)

Use 4d headless brads to secure the horizontal dividers to the carcase. There's no need to nail the vertical dividers to the carcase; gravity and friction are sufficient.

MAKING IT A CRATE

The fun part of this project is taking this nice carcase and turning it into a packing crate. You do this by nailing on 1x battens so they look a bit like rails and stiles. There is no other joinery between the battens—just glue and nails.

Cut the battens to the sizes shown in the cutlist. The easy way to install these is to first attach them to the carcase sides, trim the pieces flush to the top and bottom of the case, then finish up the work on the top and bottom.

The important thing to remember is that the battens should extend out ½"

EXPLODED VIEW

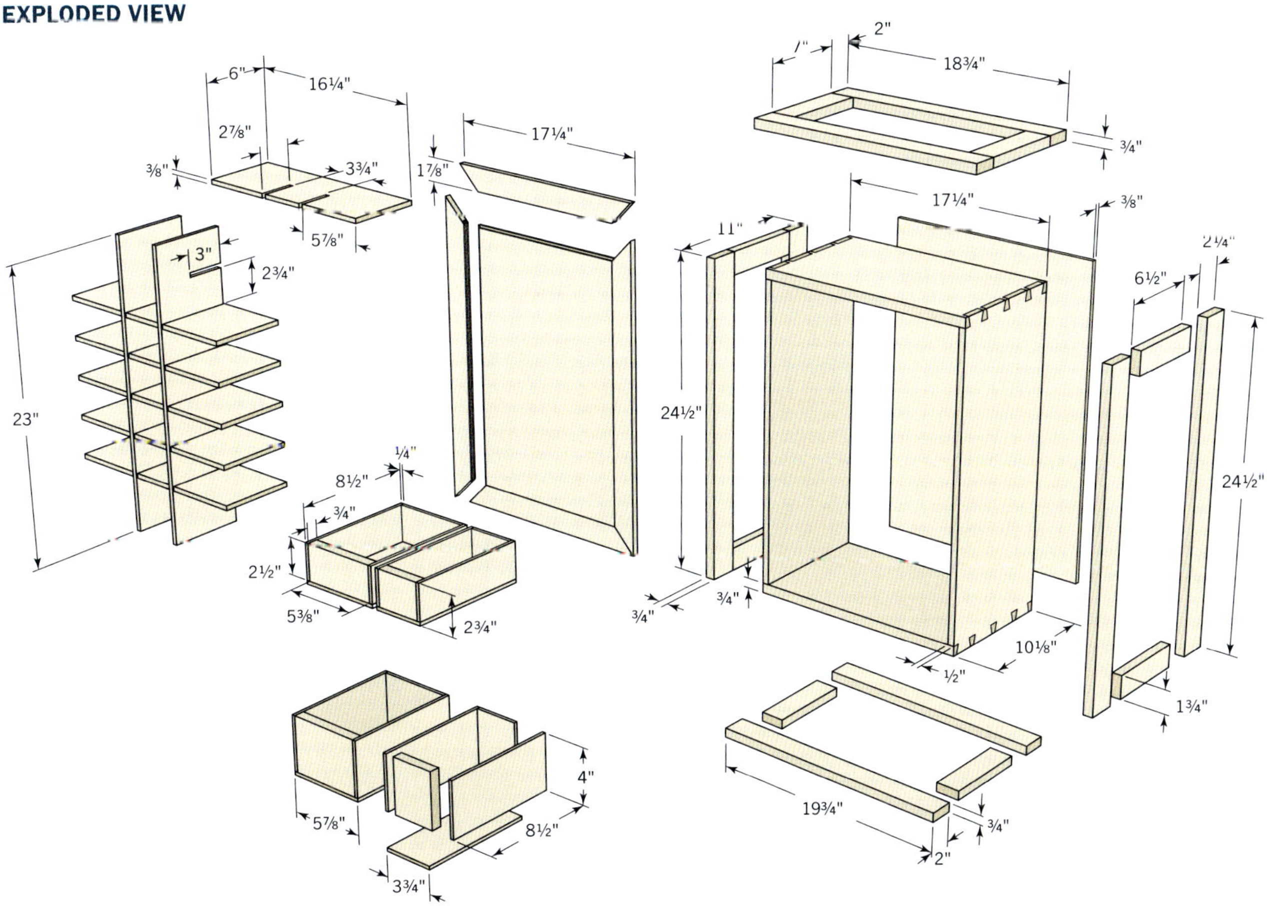

Piece by piece. The battens form the rails and stiles that frame the exterior walls of the crate. As on the original, they are simply nailed and glued to the carcase—there's no joinery between the rails and stiles. So this is fast work.

Inaccurate. The 45° setting on my iron miter box is off by about half a degree. But I don't mind. That's because I shoot my miters, which allows me to sneak up on the perfect length and angle.

Nail the miters. A single nail through the stile and into the rail prevents things from sliding around as you clamp up this mitered joint. This was, by the way, how the original door was assembled.

(or a tad more) from the front lip of the carcase. This ½" lip creates the opening for the door. Before you attach the battens, make sure their position works with the hinges you have purchased for the door. If the hinge leaf is wider than ½" you have to shift the battens forward a little on the case so the hinge can open and close.

All the battens are attached with brads and glue.

MITERED DOOR

With all the battens attached, you can determine the final sizes of your rails and stiles for the frame-and-panel door. The corners of this light-duty door are joined by miters that are glued and nailed, just like the original.

When I cut miters, I saw them first, then trim them to a perfect length and a perfect 45° with a miter shooting board and a handplane.

Even if you love your chop saw, I encourage you to give this a try sometime. I've found no easier way to cut perfect miters. By shooting the miters with a handplane, you can control the length of your rails and stiles in .001" increments. And you can hit dead-on 45° with ease.

Once the miters are cut, plow a 3⁄16"-wide x 3⁄16"-deep groove on the inside edge of the rails and stiles. The 3⁄8"-thick panel fits into the groove thanks to a rabbet cut on all four edges of the panel. Be sure to size the panel so it has a little room for expansion and contraction in its width.

I don't own any fancy clamps for gluing mitered corners—most band clamps are fairly frustrating to use—so I glue up miters, corner by corner.

First, I spread a little glue on the two mating surfaces of the miter and let them dry for a minute. Then I add more glue to the joint. I press the two pieces together and drive a single nail through the stile and into the rail.

I repeat this process for each corner (don't forget to slide the panel into the frame before adding the last piece). Then, I clamp up the joints using four ordinary bar clamps. The nails prevent the miters from sliding as you apply pressure at the corners.

TWENTY-ONE DRAWERS

Because this is a cabinet for nails, it's appropriate that the drawers are nailed together. All the drawers are constructed in a simple manner: The front and back are captured by the sides. The bottom is then nailed on.

The drawers look a little odd—the end grain of the sides and bottom is visible on the drawer front. But they are acceptable for a piece of shop furniture—and the drawers in the original have survived many years of use.

Begin by fitting all the drawer parts for each opening. I try to do as much fitting as I can before assembly. This usually means the drawer will require little or no tweaking after assembly. First, I fit each bottom to its opening. Then, I fit the sides, front, and bottom. Next, I begin assembling the drawer.

To do so, place the front and sides in position on the bottom. Feel if the drawer front needs to be reduced in length so the sides are flush to the bottom. If you need to trim the drawer front, trim the back by the same amount.

Glue and nail the sides to the front. Then, glue and nail the back to the sides. Finally, glue and nail the bottom to the drawer. Fit each drawer to its opening, numbering the drawer and its opening as you go.

HARDWARE & FINISH

As on the original, I used bin pulls for the larger drawers and knobs for the smaller drawers in the center. To ensure I got the bin pulls located correctly, I made a quick drilling jig that I clamped to each drawer front. The jig ensured I didn't make a layout error.

Begin with the bottom. Get each bottom board to slide in and out of its opening before sizing the other drawer parts. If the bottom binds, the assembled drawer will bind.

Glue the bottom. Because the parts are all softwood, which doesn't move much once it's dry, you can get away with both gluing and nailing this cross-grain joint.

Too long? Dry-assemble the drawer to feel if the drawer front is too long.

Shoot it. If the drawer front is too long, shoot it to perfect length with a plane on a shooting board. Count your strokes. Reduce the length of the drawer back by the same number of strokes, provided your original lengths were the same.

The knobs are located dead center in the fronts of the smaller drawers.

Were I to make changes to this cabinet, it would be with the hardware. While I like the bin pulls, it would be more helpful to have pulls like an old library card catalog; the card could tell you what type of fastener is inside the drawer.

To solve this problem, Roy simply wrote what is in each drawer on the bin pull. I think he did it with pencil—it's almost impossible to see on camera.

Another thought: Add 2" of depth to the cabinet and you can hang hammers, screwdrivers, and other accoutrements of fastening and unfastening on the inside of the door.

Install the hinges and knob on the door. I used a magnetic catch to hold the door shut. Because I'm the only person who works in my shop, there's no need for a lock.

I finished the nail cabinet with two coats of garnet shellac, sanding between the coats. The cabinet hangs on my shop wall with a French cleat made from ½"-thick material.

Insurance. When I have to do something 14 times, you can bet I'm going to make a jig to ensure my mind doesn't wander and cause me to make a fatal error at this stage of the project. This simple jig locates the holes for the bin pulls in the correct place. For the taller drawers on the bottom, I set the jig ⅜" lower on the drawer front.

CUT LIST & MATERIALS

	NO.	ITEM	DIMENSIONS (INCHES)			MATERIAL
			T	W	L	
□	2	Sides	½	10⅛	24½	Pine
□	2	Top & bottom	¾	10⅛	17¼	Pine
□	1	Back	⅜	17¼	24½	Pine
□	2	Door rails	½	1⅞	17¼	Pine
□	2	Door stiles	½	1⅞	24½	Pine
□	1	Door panel	⅜	13¾	21⅛	Pine
TOP FRAME						
□	2	Stiles	¾	2	18¾	Pine
□	2	Rails	¾	2	7	Pine
SIDE FRAMES						
□	4	Stiles	¾	2¼	24½	Pine
□	4	Rails	¾	1¾	6½	Pine
BOTTOM FRAME						
□	1	Front stile	¾	2	19¾	Pine
□	1	Rear stile	¾	2	18¾	Pine
□	2	Rails	¾	2	7	Pine
INTERIOR						
□	2	Vertical dividers	⅜	6	23	Pine
□	6	Horizontal dividers	⅜	6	16¼	Pine
□	12	Wide drawer fronts (& backs)	¾ (¼)	2½	5⅜	Pine
□	12	Wide drawer bottoms	¼	5⅞	8½	Pine
□	6	Narrow drawer fronts (& backs)	¾ (¼)	2½	3¼	Pine
□	6	Narrow drawer bottoms	¼	3¾	8½	Pine
□	36	Top drawer sides	¼	2½	8½	Pine
□	2	Wide lower drawer fronts (& backs)	¾ (¼)	4	5⅜	Pine
□	2	Wide lower drawer bottoms	¼	6⅜	8½	Pine
□	1	Narrow lower drawer front (& back)	¾ (¼)	4	3¼	Pine
□	1	Narrow lower drawer bottoms	¼	3¾	8½	Pine
□	6	Lower drawer sides	¼	4	8½	Pine
SUPPLIES						
□	1	Knob	–	17 mm	15 mm	Antique brass
□	2	Fixed-butt pin hinges	–	1 ¼	2	Brass
□	7	Flat knobs	–	1 ¼	1	Antique brass
□	14	Shell pulls	3 ⅛	–	–	Antique brass
□	1	Magnetic catch				

ILLUSION CABINET

Stylish legs and a dapper door dress up a simple case piece—and help to deceive the eye.

BY GARY ROGOWSKI

This design is inspired by a taper, but I needed to establish the right proportions to flesh the idea out. In much of my design work, I hover around the safe ground of a 3:5 or a 2:3 proportion in the neighborhood of Golden proportions.

For this cabinet, I thought if I were to make the eye search a bit, then a more distinct ratio was in order. Throughout the design, from the overall dimensions of the case to the size of the parts of the door, everything was held as close as possible to 1:2. This made for noticeable changes in shapes both in the overall form of the piece and in its members.

SIMPLIFIED CONSTRUCTION

The cabinet appears to be frame-and-panel construction with the legs proud of the side panels. But the sides are solid with the legs simply glued on.

To yield 13" in width, I assembled the sides from two mahogany boards. I finished planing and sanding both panels then cut them to final length before gluing on the 1⁄16"-overlong legs, which are also mahogany. It's a bit easier to manage cleanup this way.

I milled the legs, cut the taper on the bandsaw, and cleaned the faces on

Downhill. After cutting the tapers on the legs with the bandsaw, remove any mill marks using a jack plane.

Alignment. Biscuits aren't needed to strengthen this joint, but they help keep the two legs and the panel aligned during assembly.

Time well spent. It takes time and attention to detail to make the template, but the results are worth the effort.

Square corners. A sharp chisel squares the rounded corners left by the router.

the jointer. A pass or two with my jack plane took out any milling marks and I was almost ready for gluing. I used my biscuit joiner to register the panel faces and legs.

Once the legs are glued on, you treat the sides like a flat panel. Plane or sand them dead flat first, then mortise for the bottom panel.

I made a mortising template to cut my mortises. Using a template guide and ¼" straight bit in my plunge router, I routed the ½"-deep x ⅝"-wide mortises and chopped the corners square with my chisel.

I routed the shoulders of the tenons on the router table, making sure to have a backer piece in place to prevent blowout on the back edge of the cut. These tenons are about 1⁄16" shorter in length than the mortise depth to allow for excess glue.

Cut the top rails to the same length as the bottom panel. Cut a 1⁄16" shoulder on the bottom face of each rail to match the bottom's tenon length. This guarantees identical shoulder-to-shoulder length for the top and bottom. The shoulder is used to register the parts for marking.

Stand the bottom panel in place on a side and make sure the front edges align. With a pencil, mark the mortise locations onto the bottom. With only a few tenons to cut, it's quicker to cut them by hand than on a machine. (I tried at the table saw—it was too fussy.)

After I marked out the tenon sides, I clamped the bottom panel low in the vise to eliminate vibration, then sawed down to define the tenons. I used my bandsaw to carefully remove the waste.

Fit the tenons starting at one edge and work your way across. Having a good shoulder plane makes a huge difference in your ability to finesse a fit. Chamfer the tenon ends as well to make sliding them home a bit easier.

The top rails sit flat to the tops of the side panels. I used half-blind dovetails for this joinery because they're invisible and strong.

Three-step tenons. Cut the tenon shoulders at the router table, then define each tenon cheek with straight cuts using a handsaw. The waste in between is removed at the bandsaw.

Trim & fit. Start at the front and work toward the back to fit the tenons in the bottom panel.

The top rails were first cut as long as the bottom panel. After I made the shoulders, I cut off ⅛" to keep the tails from being too close to the outer face of the panel. There's no point in risking a crack with too tight a fit. I used a 1:6 slope to lay out the dovetails and cut them at the bench before marking out the sockets on the panels.

To mark the pinboard, I put the bottom panel into the sides and clamped things tight. Before marking the pin position, I set the top rails in place and clamped those as well—the small shoulders make it easy to clamp across the case. I used a marking knife for this, but somewhere along the way I lost my ability to see tiny knife marks in end grain. To darken them, I used a drafting pencil sharpened to a fine point; it worked great. After sawing inside the lines, I used a chisel to complete the sockets for the tails.

Tails on top. After adjusting the length of the top rails, cut the dovetails. With the rail in place, mark the sockets.

Saw then chop. Define the edges of the tail sockets with two saw cuts. Chisel out the waste.

THINK AHEAD ABOUT THE DOOR

With the rail dovetails fit into the top of the case sides, it's time to lay out the knife hinges. First, make sure the front edges of the case are all trued up. I clamped the cabinet onto my bench and planed the edges flush.

Make the mortises for these hinges before assembly to keep your life simple. The Brusso knife hinges I used have a brass washer on the pin that separates the two leaves. This sets the reveals or gaps for all the door edges. I made shims out of plastic laminate and a piece of masking tape to match the thickness of the washer.

Put one shim against the case side to set the gap of the hinge stile then mark for the hinge leaf with a marking gauge and knife. I use a router to ensure a consistent depth on the leaf mortises, then chop the corners square. It's easier to drill for the screw holes now as well. I drilled and ran in steel pilot screws with some wax on the threads to lead the way. I can install my brass screws later on with no worries about breaking a screw.

This cabinet has only two shelves, and I like the ease that adjustable shelves give in building a piece. You just have to remember to get the holes drilled before gluing up. I made a template out of ¼" MDF and marked hole centers for shelf pins exactly where I wanted each shelf to be.

To give me options for shelf placement, I made marks 1" higher and lower than my layout. Using a brad point bit, I drilled the template, then placed it inside the assembled case, marked the holes with the same bit, then deepened those marks with an awl.

These marks are easy to see and align at the drill press. Set up an auxiliary table to support the case side. Shim under the case sides to keep the tapered legs off the table (this also helps to ensure that the holes are drilled straight).

Before glue-up, I cut grooves for the kick piece that goes under the case bottom. I marked the stop point of each groove on the sides, then used my plunge router with a ⅜"-diameter bit and a fence to cut a ¼"-deep groove. I used a chisel to chop the ends of the stopped cuts square.

PLAN

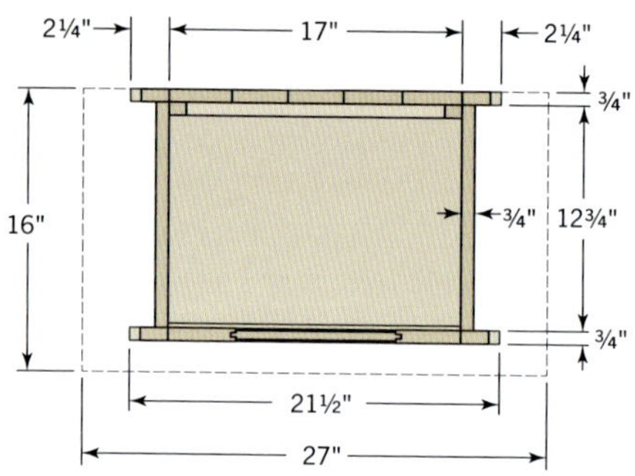

FRONT

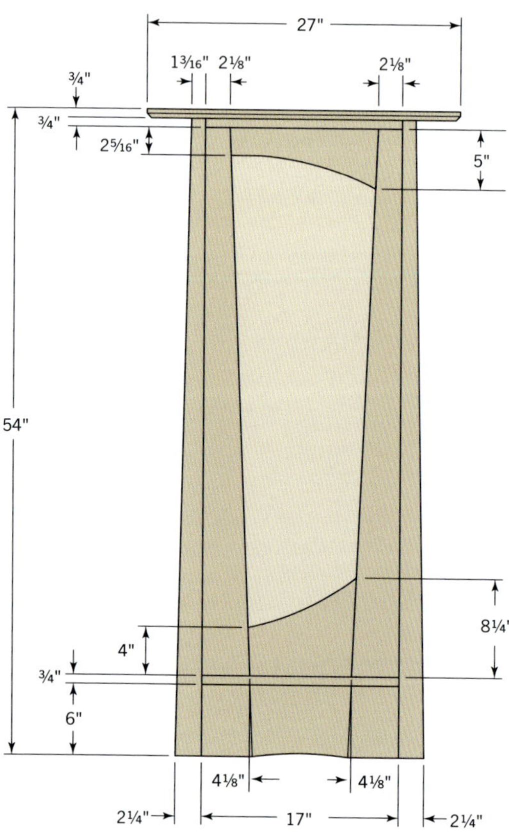

BACK

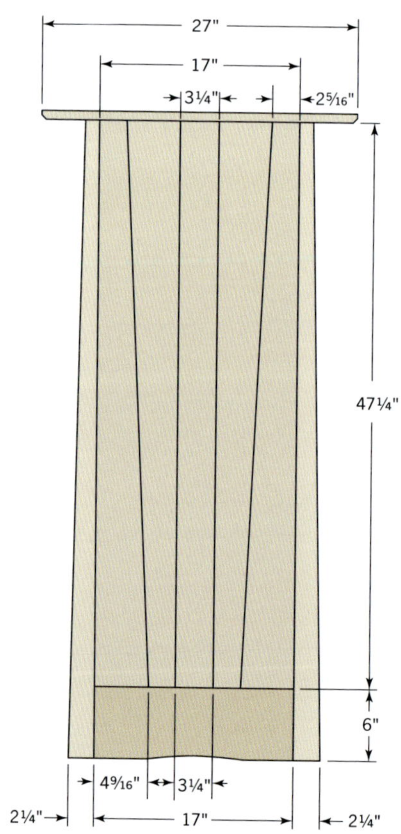

SECTION

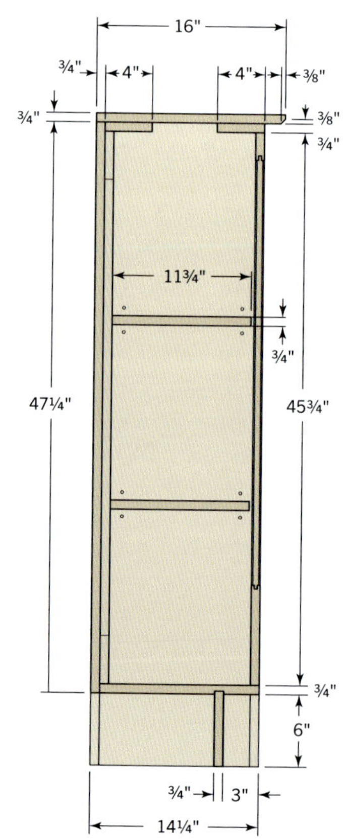

GET IT TOGETHER

As with any cabinet project, assembly is a calming and soothing balm after a long day's work. Right. How I wish that were true. Glue changes everything. Here is what I learned (again) from the experience: You have to plan your glue-up, get your clamps, and have clamps and corner blocks ready to pull the cabinet square. Assume the worst and be happily disappointed if it doesn't occur. It's much better than assuming that everything will go right, then frantically trying to fix a problem with the glue drying.

I made clamping cauls out of some clear 2x4 scrap laying about. I put a slight convex curve on one edge using a bandsaw, then smoothed the curve with a handplane. The cauls fit between the legs of the side panels. Two deep extension *F*-style clamps hold things tight. The cauls pulled the tenons in fine, and the shoulders closed up great.

DETAILED DOOR

The door frame is made of tapered stiles and shaped rails. The parts all taper from the wide to the narrow ends by a factor of two. This gives the door a distinct look, but makes for challenging construction because none of the frame joints are square.

I made a cardboard template of the taper for the stiles. That allowed me to visualize the slope and mark an identical angle on both pieces. I cut the tapers at the bandsaw, then removed the saw marks with a plane.

Loose- or slip-tenon joints are the simplest way to build this door. Cut all your parts to size, taper the long door stiles, then cut the angles and curves on the rails. (See p. 116, "Center of the Universe.") I made corrections for both length and angle where needed using a low-angle jack plane to fine-tune the fit.

I then mortised all the parts for the loose tenons. It's much easier to make

Pattern match. The cardboard template ensures that the tapers on the door stiles are identical.

Tapered rip. The bandsaw is ideal for cutting the tapers on the door stiles.

Joinery last. After the door parts are adjusted to fit, use loose tenons to join the rails and stiles.

Rough & ready. Use a wire brush to add texture to the front of the panel.

CENTER OF THE UNIVERSE

Open cabinets, with no fixed shelves and only a door across the front, can twist on an uneven floor. This is especially true when the cabinet is loaded with books or bottles or both. My strategy is to build them on a flat and true surface that becomes the Center of the Universe.

When the piece goes to its final home and the door doesn't close right or the reveals have changed, I can say: "When I built this piece, it was built at the Center of the Universe and built square—so it's the floor that's the problem." Then I can shim the case under the legs to make the door fit perfectly again.

One at a time. Fitting the pieces to each corner makes it easier to achieve a nice-fitting door. Loose joinery makes this possible.

After the case is glued, I set it on an assembly platform. This platform was double-checked to see that its not twisted because my shop floor is anything but flat. I placed winding sticks on top and adjusted with shims underneath the platform to pull it in true. Now I had a working area that I could trust.

I checked the bottom rail and the hinge stile of my door against my door opening. If the door is out of square, adjust it to fit. You want to have enough room to place shims under the door and against the hinge side of the case. I used a jack plane to fit the door to its opening.

Detail work. With most of the door edges chamfered, a bit of work on the rail ends continues the detail as it highlights the joint.

any adjustments when there are no tenons protruding from the rails.

Once I had the door frame put together dry, I planed all my parts flat then set up a router with a slot cutter to make the groove for the panel. I prefer to cut straight into the dry-assembled door rather than separately into its parts. The panel grooves will line up better this way.

The door frame is ¾" thick, so I cut a ¼"-wide x ⅜"-deep groove for the ½"-thick panel. I marked out the shape of the door onto a glued-up fir panel and added 5⁄16" all around for tongues that fit into the grooves. At the router table, I rabbeted both faces of the panel to make my ¼"-thick tongue.

I cut the rabbet on the outside of the panel then planed, scraped, and sanded it. To add texture to the panel's front face, I scrubbed it with a wire brush, then cut the second rabbet and fine-tuned the fit of the panel with my shoulder plane. A coat of shellac was applied to the panel before the door was glued up.

I fit the bottom door rail and hinge stile to the case, then mortised in the lower knife hinge. I fit the top rail before putting in the top knife hinge. The handle stile is fitted next with a 5° back-bevel on the edge of the door so it clears the case when opening.

FINISHING TOUCHES

The kick is the last piece to get glued in place. I fit it to the grooves in the sides and bottom of the case so it is a slide-in fit. Check for the high spots that show shiny on the tongue and plane those with a shoulder plane until the kick fits home.

The kick has a taper detail carved into it. With the door in place, I marked the taper line of the stiles onto the case then transferred this down to the kick. I pulled out the piece and with a *V*-chisel

Tapered, too. To continue the overall design, the outer slats of the back are also tapered.

In reverse. The shape of the handle tapers in the opposite direction of the stile. Brass pins provide an accent to the darker wood.

CUT LIST & MATERIALS

	NO.	ITEM	DIMENSIONS (INCHES) T	W	L	MATERIAL	COMMENTS
☐	4	Legs	¾	2¼	53¼	Mahogany	Tapered
☐	2	Sides	¾	12¾	53¼	Mahogany	
☐	1	Bottom panel	¾	12¾	18	Mahogany	
☐	2	Shelves	¾	11¾	16⅞	Mahogany	
☐	1	Top	¾	16	27	Mahogany	
☐	2	Top rails	¾	4	18	Mahogany	
☐	2	Back cleats	¾	¾	45¾	Mahogany	
☐	1	Straight back plank	¾	3¼	47¼	Redwood	*
☐	4	Tapered back planks	¾	4⁹⁄₁₆	47¼	Redwood	*
☐	1	Kick	¾	6¼	17½	Mahogany	
☐	2	Door stiles	¾	4⅛	45¾	Mahogany	Tapered
☐	1	Top door rail	¾	5	12¾	Mahogany	Curved
☐	1	Bottom door rail	¾	8¼	9¼	Mahogany	Curved
☐	1	Door panel	½	13⅜	39⁷⁄₁₆	Fir	Shaped to opening**
☐	2	Offset pivot knife hinges	⁵⁄₁₆	¾	3¼	Brass	
☐	1	Handle	¾	¾	4	Ebony	

*Back planks have shiplapped edges; **Door panel size determined by adding ⅝" to opening in dry-assembled door frame to account for the grooves.

carved the lines before gluing the kick into the case, then cut a slight arch between the *V*-grooves on the bottom edge of the kick for visual interest.

The top is two pieces of mahogany glued up. A 45° bevel is added to the ends and front edge; leave the back edge square. I then planed a gentle bullnose to relieve the sharp edges. The top is screwed to the case through the top rails after finishing.

The back is made of five tapered redwood slats. The central slat is straight, but the outer slats are tapered and have overlapping rabbets. With the top rail and bottom panel set in the thickness of the attached legs, I screwed each of the back slats to them, top and bottom. I added cleats on the inside of the sides just to cover up any movement issues of the back slats.

The door handle is a piece of ebony with three brass escutcheon pins put in to brighten it up a bit. It's attached to the door with a pair of loose tenons. The catch is a brass three-way ball catch.

My cabinets have an inside finish of shellac. On the outside, to darken the wood, I used a coat of linseed oil and let that cure for several days. Six coats of shellac were applied and rubbed out, then I waxed the cabinet.

For the inside of a case, you can also scent the shellac. It's astonishing when you open the door to a pleasant smell if you choose the right scent. Avoid patchouli. Vanilla or lavender would be good. I mix 4 ounces of shellac and 20 drops of scented oil. That yields a delightful surprise when you open up the case. It's good to keep the oil around to brighten up the scent over time.

PLEASANT HILL CLASSIC CUPBOARD

Common wood from a common source creates an uncommon beauty.

BY KERRY PIERCE

I began my study of the Shaker furniture at Pleasant Hill, Ky., with a quick survey of the contents of the enormous Centre Family Dwelling, sticking my head in the door of each room, making a mental note of everything that caught my eye: a table here, a chair there, a little blanket chest, a tripled clothes hanger.

Each item on my mental list had something about it that set it apart from other objects in the Dwelling. In some cases, it was a splash of color, in others a bit of intriguing joinery, in others a form that deviated from Shaker norms. In this manner, I chugged along for maybe half an hour; looking, storing, and getting excited about the prospect of looking more closely later on.

Then, in a room on the second floor, I saw this cupboard hanging from a peg rail above a wash stand. I stuck my head in, caught my breath, released it, and then slowly entered the room. The cupboard was familiar (Christian Becksvoort's book *The Shaker Legacy*), but I had forgotten about it. I know I wasn't expecting to see it there.

I stepped over the low railing erected to keep the public at a distance. (I had permission from the curator.) I stuck my nose close to the piece to study the pegs that penetrated the joinery of the frame-and-panel door, then backed off. This was something special, something profoundly Shaker, something that—unlike many pieces in the Pleasant Hill collection—could never be attributed to country origins.

The editors at *Popular Woodworking* had sent me and the magazine's photographer, Al Parrish, to the Shaker Village to write and illustrate a couple of articles about Western Shaker construction methods and design.

Nobody told me to do any measured drawings, but when I took the job, I was pretty sure I'd end up drawing at least a few pieces, and as soon as I saw this cupboard, "pretty sure" changed to dead certain.

MATERIAL FROM A HOME CENTER

I usually buy lumber from hardwood dealers—businesses that typically require a 100 board feet (bf) minimum order. So I can't buy, for instance, 75 bf of curly maple or 50 bf of cherry. In most cases, I don't mind these minimums. I

Pilot. Although it's possible to drive nails into "green" hardwood without pre-drilling, thoroughly dry hardwood requires pre-drilled holes—that is, if you want to avoid split stock. The through hole should be nearly the same diameter as the shank of the nail. The hole that penetrates the second piece of stock should be a bit smaller in order to give the material a good grip on the nail.

Place the shelf. Tap the shelf into its dados using a protective block of scrap.

Level the edges. Use a plane to level the edges of the cupboard's case before you attach the face frame.

Make the bead. Although the bead on the Shaker original was likely made with a scratch stock (because there is evidence of this tool everywhere at Pleasant Hill), I chose an 1/8" side-bead plane.

always need cherry, walnut, and curly maple. But sometimes, I don't really want 100 bf of a particular species, and anyone buying small lots of hardwood at stores catering to woodworking hobbyists will find he needs the support of a full-time cardiologist when checking out at the cash register. I've been experimenting with another source for poplar: my local home-center store. All the big home-center stores charge more per board foot than hardwood dealers. But there are some good reasons to consider these type of suppliers for poplar (and pine).

For one thing, the material has been surfaced, and let's face it: One of the

CUT LIST & MATERIALS

	NO.	ITEM	DIMENSIONS (INCHES)			MATERIAL	COMMENTS
			T	W	L		
☐	1	Top	3/8	7 1/2	31 7/8	Poplar	
☐	1	Bottom	13/16	7 1/2	32	Poplar	Stock can be slightly oversize
☐	2	Sides	13/16	5 7/8	17 13/16	Poplar	
☐	1	Face frame top rail	13/16	2 7/16	20	Poplar	
☐	1	Face frame bottom rail	13/16	1 7/8	20	Poplar	
☐	2	Face frame stiles	13/16	5 7/16	17 13/16	Poplar	
☐	2	Sub top & bottom	7/8	5 7/8	29 1/4	Poplar	
☐	1	Shelf	3/4	5 7/8	30	Poplar	In 3/4"x 3/8" d. dados
☐	2	Door rails	13/16	2 7/8	16 1/8	Poplar	2" tenons on each end
☐	2	Door stiles	13/16	3 15/16	13 1/2	Poplar	
☐	1	Door panel	5/16	8 5/8	13	Poplar	1/16" gap all around
☐	2	Hangers	5/16	2 7/8	27	Poplar	
☐		Backboards	5/16	30 7/8	17 13/16	Poplar	Random widths to fill 30 7/8"
☐	1	Knob*	1	1	1 11/16	Walnut	
☐	1	Catch	1/4	7/16	3/4	Walnut	
☐	2	Hinges**			1 3/4	Brass	

* I made the knob 1/8" longer than the original knob. This was a mistake, one I didn't notice until I prepared the materials list. The extra length is in the long cove. The length I give in the materials list is the length of the Shaker original to match the drawing.

** The hinges on my reproduction also are historically inaccurate. The hinges on the original are 1 3/4" long (as they appear on my drawing). Here, too, I made a mistake. I marked and mortised for a pair of 2"-long hinges.

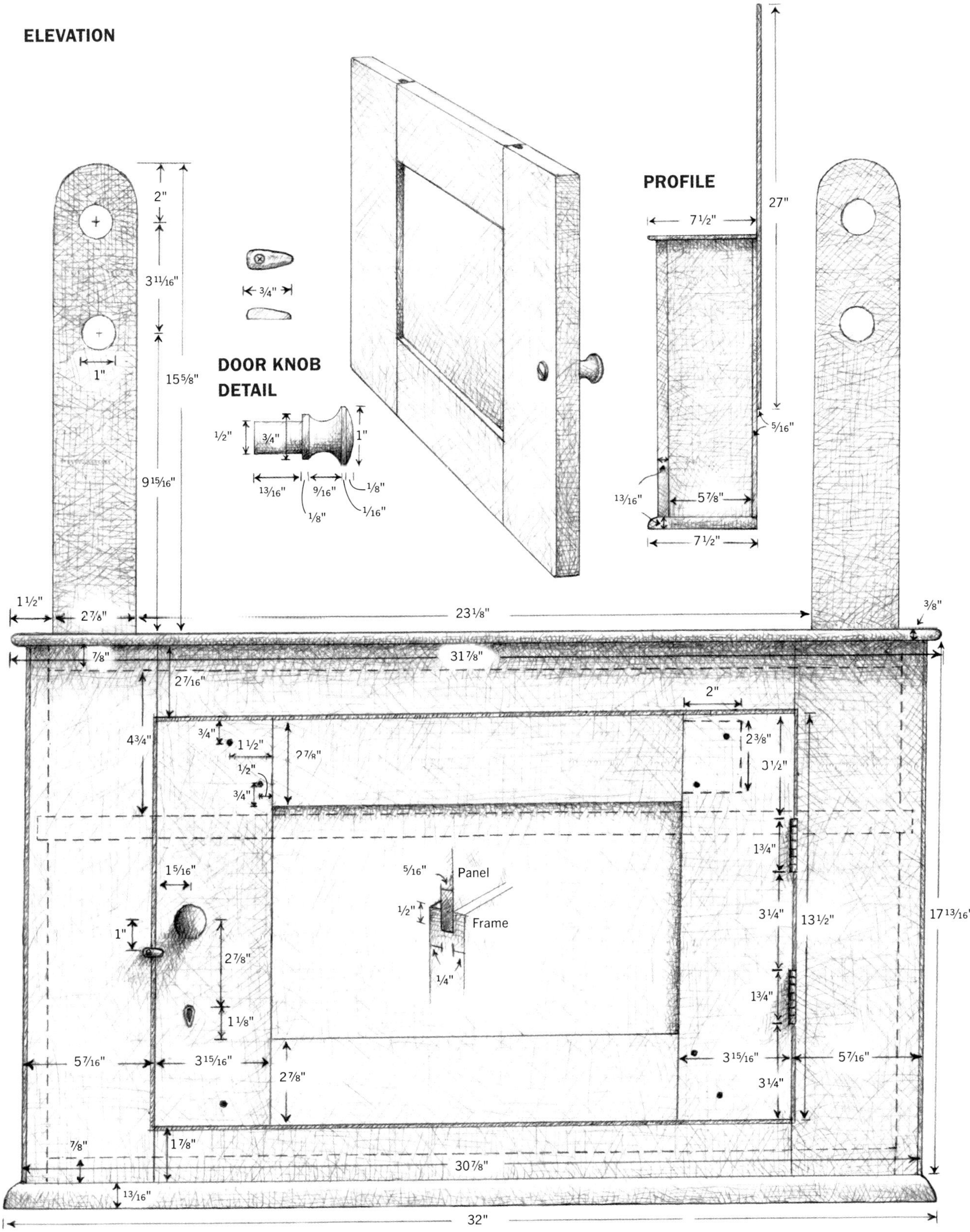

ILLUSTRATION BY THE AUTHOR

more odious chores is flattening and thicknessing material. But here's a more important reason: I can buy only perfect boards. If there's a knot, a split, a bit of wane—I don't buy it. If it's not perfectly flat—and I mean billiard-table flat—I put it back.

Try that with a hardwood dealer. He might let you set aside a few boards with egregious defects, but if you reject eight boards out of ten, he might decide he doesn't want your business after all.

In fact, I have developed the habit of buying all my secondary wood this way. Every time I go to the store, I sort through all the poplar and clear white pine, and I buy every perfect board. This little cupboard is built of poplar I'd culled from the home-center's stock over the previous month.

ASSEMBLING THE CASE

I chose to use 8d coated nails to assemble the cupboard because the nail heads visible on the original are about the size of 8d nail heads, and I knew 8d nails, which are 2½" long, would result in a solid construction. Eight penny nails are big for this application, and I think you could have good results with a 7d nail as well, but I wouldn't recommend anything smaller than that.

Initially, the whole nail thing made me uncomfortable. I've spent too many years cutting wood-to-wood joinery to embrace this (sacrilegious?) method of work. But early in the construction process, I had to remove a piece I'd nailed in the wrong location, and let's just say I'm convinced this little cupboard will never come apart.

These nails require the drilling of two holes. The first is a through hole in the board you're nailing through. This hole should be just large enough for the shank of an 8d penny nail to pass without being driven by your hammer.

The second hole should be the full length of your 8d nail and just a bit smaller than the shank of the nail. It has to be small enough so that you have to drive the nail in with your hammer but not so small that seating the nail results in split material. Experiment on scrap before you work on the good stuff.

If you look at the top photo on page 119, you'll see me drilling the smaller hole in a partially assembled joint. The drill for the larger through hole sits on the bench behind me.

After nailing the carcase together, fit the shelf and tap it into its dados.

The original cupboard has only one shelf, although there are dados for two equally spaced shelves. I thought that an interior divided into only two compartments, instead of three, made more sense on this modest-sized cupboard, so I eliminated the second shelf the original cupboard had at birth. This gave me a fairly small compartment above and a larger compartment below.

After the shelf has been nailed into place, level the cabinet front and back with a plane.

The cupboard has ⅛" beads along each of the front corners and around the door frame. The beads on the corners are cut on both the front and side of the vertical parts of the cupboard front. This produces a bead that's visible from either perspective.

If you haven't used a molding plane, an ⅛" side-bead plane (p. 120, right) is a great place to start. You can find these relatively common planes at flea markets, antique malls, and, of course,

A little more work. The junction of the horizontal and vertical beads must be completed with a little paring chisel work.

Nail it together. Carefully drive the nails that attach the face frame. (If you miss and ding up your stock, don't despair. Just spoon a bit of water onto the ding. As the fibers swell to accept the water, the surface of the wood will return to its original configuration.)

Shape the edge. Bench planes can be made to do a fair amount of edge shaping. Here, I'm using a bench plane to create the radius between a line drawn on the edge and a line drawn on the top of the cupboard bottom.

Make the mortises. These narrow, deep mortises can be tricky to chop with hand tools.

online. But you must be sure to purchase a plane with a reasonably straight sole. Some have bowed beyond repair in the century and a half since their creation. "Reasonably" straight, however, doesn't mean "perfectly" straight. This little ⅛" side-bead plane I'm using here has a bit of a bow but it still works fine.

Unlike most molding planes, which are designed to be held at an angle (the spring angle), side-bead planes are designed to be held upright, their sides perpendicular to the surfaces being worked. Set the iron so that it's barely visible when you sight along the sole of the plane, tap the wedge firm, then crowd the plane's fence against the edge of the work and push the plane forward. If you have the right amount of iron exposed, a tiny shaving will squirt out the side of the plane. (Test the plane's setting on scrap before working on the cupboard stock. A rank iron—one set too deep—can tear out the bead.) After a half dozen passes, you will have defined a little bead and quirk.

If you prefer routers, there are ⅛" bead cutters available that will simulate the work of this plane.

Cutting the bead around the door on the face frame stiles of the cupboard front requires a little trickery because you simply can't do it with a properly set up side-bead plane. This is because the bead doesn't run all the way to the ends of the boards on the face-frame stiles (although the bead does run from end to end on the face-frame rails so these beads can be cut in the way I'm demonstrating here.)

Caveat: The Shaker maker might have done this with a scratch stock. A scratch stock is nothing more than two pieces of scrap wood between which is sandwiched a small bit of metal filed to the necessary profile. The wood part of the scratch stock provides a way to hold the metal at the necessary angle without damaging the craftsman's fingers (it also stabilizes the metal), while the metal cuts the bead with a scraping action. It's simple but effective when properly sharpened.

You can, however, cut the stopped bead on the face-frame stiles of the cabinet front with a side-bead plane if you cheat a little. Tap the iron down so that it hangs an extra ⅛" or so from the sole of the plane. That will allow the iron to engage the work when the sole of the plane is not riding down on the bead you're cutting. You are, in effect, using the side-bead plane as a beading tool. This too is something you should experiment with on scrap before trying it out on the good stuff.

Nail the components of the face frame into place.

After the frame has been attached, you'll then finish the bead around the door with a paring chisel (p. 122, left), followed by sandpaper.

The cupboard top and bottom both have radiused edges. The top has a 180° radius, the bottom only a 90° radius These radii can be formed with molding planes (or roundover bits in a router), but I've always made this shape with a bench plane. You'll be amazed at how quickly you can do this work—much more quickly than you could set up a router to perform the same operation, and of course working with a plane means no dust and no noise. The shop remains quiet enough so you can plan the next few steps in the construction process.

Pre-glue layout. Before you glue up the door, lay out the parts and make certain that they will all come together during glue-up.

Riven pegs. Riven pegs are not only historically accurate, they are also stronger than sawn pegs because they eliminate the possibility of grain run-out.

If you choose my method, you'll first need some pencil lines to plane between. One of these lines should identify the midpoint of the board's edge. The other line should be placed on an adjacent surface a distance from the edge that is equal to half the thickness of the board.

To create the radius, simply remove shavings in the area between these lines until, working by eye, you've established the rounded edge.

You should create the radii on the ends of the board before tackling the long-grain radius to avoid tear out at the corners.

Nail the shiplapped backboards onto the back of the carcase. Nail the top and bottom in place.

MAKING THE DOOR

The cabinet took me maybe three hours to assemble. The door took a day and a half to build and fit. In part, this is because the door is the only element with any traditional joinery, but primarily, it was because doors require a lot of careful fitting.

The original door has ¼"-thick x 2"-wide x 4"-long through tenons on the rails. And so did the first door I made for this particular reproduction.

But the mortises must have been a little out of whack because when I assembled the door, it had an unacceptable amount of twist, a result probably of an incorrectly cut mortise. This is something that's easy to do when chopping long and very thin mortises by hand. So I made a second door, this time with mortises only 2" deep. These were much easier to cut accurately, and a tightly fit 2"-long tenon has more than enough glue surface for this door, particularly when the glue joints are reinforced with ¼" walnut pegs.

The photo at the top of the page shows the door components before the door was glued up. Notice the ¼"-wide, ½"-deep through grooves milled into all of the inside edges of the door's rails and stiles. The flat center panel floats in these grooves.

The door is opened with a turned walnut knob. I turned two knobs from the spindle shown because I had decided to make a pair of these hanging cupboards.

The final touches on the door are the ¼"-diameter pegs that reinforce each tenon. Cut off a length of walnut (or some other durable, easily split hardwood) that is a bit longer than the thickness of the door components. Then, with a wide chisel and hammer, split off squares about 5⁄16" on a side. Pare these squares into approximate rounds, holding the individual pegs as shown on page 124 (bottom).

The splits in the center of the photo are the splits from which the pegs are shaved. The pegs on the left have been shaved close to their final shapes.

Cut and shape the hangers as shown in the illustration. Nail them to the back—place the nails so you catch a shelf and the sub-top of the carcase.

FINISHING

The original cupboard was stained red, but I opted for paint in order to conceal the nail heads. I began with a coat of latex primer, which I sanded, then followed that with two coats of a "designer" red that approximated the color of the original piece.

Of course, the problem with paint is the dimensional change it causes. Each layer of paint adds measurably to the width and thickness of the part to which it's applied. A door stile that was 4" wide after sanding, might be 4⅛" wide after applying three coats of paint. So even though I had fit the door with a comfortable 1⁄16" gap all around, after painting, I had to remove the door and plane off additional width from all the rails and all the stiles and then repaint those planed edges in order to get the door to open and close properly.

My wife asked me how the Shakers might have used the original cupboard. I had to tell her I didn't know.

Because it was poplar—rather than, say, cherry or curly maple—it probably was a utility cabinet of some kind, maybe something that hung in a washroom, something that might once have held soaps or cleaning brushes, but because it was so portable—just remove it from the pegs in one room and hang it from the pegs in another—it might have had several incarnations in its original life, as the Shakers moved it from room to room to suit the needs of a community dwindling steadily in size over the years.

My wife decided to hang hers in the kitchen. She's going to fill it with spices, and then use the top surface to display her collection of antique tin cans with brightly lithographed color labels.

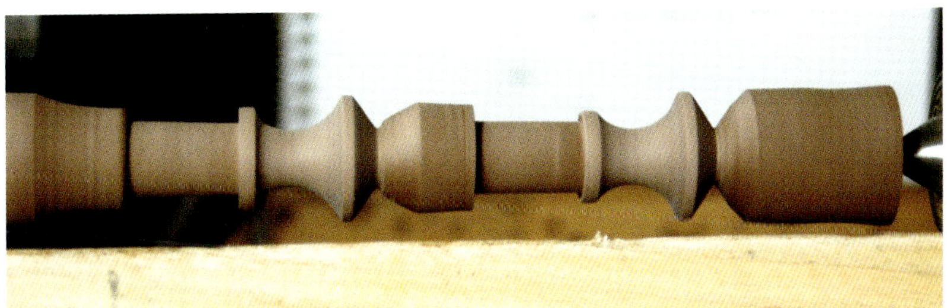

Turn the knobs. Use a skew to shape the top of the knob and a fingernail gouge to cut the cove. The tenon can be cut with a paring chisel laid flat on the rest with the bevel down.

Finish. The original cupboard had been stained. I chose to use a primer and paint combination in order to best mimic the look of the aged original finish.

CONTEMPORARY CABINET

The inspiration for this simple build hangs on a live-edge piece of walnut.

BY MEGAN FITZPATRICK

A contemporary look and no dovetails: Those were my self-imposed rules for this cabinet design. I've just completed a remodel on my kitchen, you see, with shop-built Shaker-style cabinets and a passel of hand-dovetailed drawers. I needed a change in design direction.

This walnut and spalted beech hanging cabinet is the result, and while I can certainly see some Shaker (with a touch of Krenov) in its bones, the live-edge top and mix of woods brings it into (or at least closer to) the 21st century.

Rather than relying on the cut list and illustrations provided, I urge you to let your own eye and the wood you have available guide your build. While I'm pleased with the proportions here, the depth and width were at least in part determined by the width of the walnut and beech I had available, and the place I plan to hang the cabinet.

START AT THE BOTTOM

I began by milling the walnut stock for the posts to 1½" square, leaving all the pieces 8" or so over-long. That's because I wasn't sure of the angle I wanted on the pyramid at the bottom of each, and needed some room to try out a few. I used a backsaw to rough out a variety of angles, but in the end, settled on 45°. That's an easy cut at the table saw.

Mark the pyramid base (where it transitions into the flat of the post) 1" up from the bottom on at least one face, then tilt your table saw blade to 45°. Align the saw blade at the top of the cut with your layout line, then cut all four faces. This leaves you with a ½" flat centered on the bottom of each post.

I recommend making these cuts before cutting your stock to final length (off the top, of course); that way, you have some wiggle room if you experience blow-out or decide to change the angle.

After you have a pleasing pyramid, reset your table saw blade to 0° to cut the posts to final length, then decide how you want them to appear in the finished piece. Arrange them in a bundle in the correct order and draw a cabinetmaker's triangle on the top to help keep you oriented throughout the rest of the build.

Now lay out a ¼"-wide x ¼"-deep groove on the front of the back posts and on the back of the front posts, in which ¼"-thick side panels will float. For a pleasing shadow line, I located my panels ¼" back from the edge, then made the cut with a slot cutter at the router table.

Because it won't show once the top is attached, you can run the groove out the top of the posts. At the bottom, however, set stop blocks or mark the cut termination point on the stock or the router fence and pull the workpiece away from the bit before you cut into your pyramids.

The grooves terminate into ¼"-wide x 1"-deep mortises for the rails, so mark out those mortises and get ready to deepen your grooves.

At the top, the mortises are 1" long and begin ¼" from the top of the post; at the bottom, they are 4" long, and begin ¼" up from the transition line from pyramid to flat.

I set up the hollow-chisel mortiser to cut the mortises—and the grooves make setting the chisel location simple. (Note: You could reverse these operations. Lay out and cut the mortises first—that would make it easier to set up the slot cutter at the router table and it would be easy to tell when you reached the end of the groove cut, because the bit would stop cutting.)

After the mortises for the side rails are cut, bring the work back to your bench, check the depth and clean out the trench as necessary. Leave the router setup alone; you'll need it for the doors.

Pyramid. Mark a line 1" from the end of your stock, then align the 45°-angled blade to exit the cut at that line; this results in a flat-topped pyramid. Make sure the stock is straight and square to ensure the flat is centered.

Cabinetmaker's triangle. The point that meets on the two front posts helps you to always easily see what goes where as your build progresses.

Test before cutting. A router with a slot cutter makes quick work of grooves—and it can also make quick mistakes. Test your setup on a piece of scrap sized exactly to your workpiece specs before making your actual cuts.

Chop, chop. While using the mortiser, I always keep my left hand on the wheel that moves the work right to left—that way, there's no chance I'll grab the front-to-back adjustment by mistake. And notice how I've skipped a chisel's width on my first series of cuts; leaving waste on either side helps to keep the chisel from deflecting. After making these "skip cuts" down the full length of a mortise, I work my way back to remove the remaining waste.

I used a dado stack at the table saw for the next task: the ⅝"-wide x ½"-deep rabbet on the back edges of the rear posts. Note that the rabbets terminate ½" above the top of the pyramids at the bottom of the posts, so the cut must be finished by hand at the bottom; at the other end, it's a through-cut.

The final work on the posts is to drill shelf-pin holes for two adjustable shelves. I decided on three positions for each shelf, each an inch apart, and located these on the interior post faces. With this layout, the holes and pins won't show at the front when the doors are open (and at the back, they'll be in shadow).

Measuring down from the top of the posts, I marked these at 9", 10", and 11", and 17", 18", and 19", then struck a centerline through the 1"-width of stock behind the groove. I used the drill press to ensure I ended up with perfectly straight ¼" holes.

RAILS & STILES

For the rails and stiles, straight grain gives you the most pleasing appearance, particularly if you're using a figured or spalted wood for the door panels—you don't want the panels in a visual fight with their frames. Prep the stock for the stiles and rails for both the sides and the doors at the same time. And prep a few extra lengths for machine setup.

Once you have the stock milled to ¾" thick, reassess your wood and choose the best-looking, straightest-grained pieces for the doors. If possible, cut the center door stiles from one piece of wider stock; the grain will then match perfectly in the middle.

The upper rails on both the sides and the doors are 1½" wide; the lower rails on both are 4½" wide (see the cut list for the length of each piece on my build). It's best to cut all four narrow pieces with the same saw setting, then all four wide pieces with the same setting; that way, you ensure the widths match perfectly as you move around the cabinet.

Now take one of the test pieces (you did prep extra, right?) to the router table and confirm the setup. Theoretically, the cutter should be automatically centered in the ¾" stock because you raised it to ¼" when cutting the grooves in the posts. Thus, the centered grooves in the rails and stiles align with the grooves in the posts.

Mark the face side of your test piece, then run a groove on the edge and show the test piece to a post. Do they match? Yes? Carry on. No? Try flipping the test piece; they will now.

If you are off by a little, don't raise or lower the cutter—what matters is not that these grooves are perfectly centered, but that they match the grooves in the posts. So take note of which face should be toward the table, mark those on the rails and stiles, then run a through-groove on the inside edge of the eight rails, and a stopped groove on the four door stiles. (Note that if you're persnickety, you could reset an

Finish by hand. No matter what machine or tool you use to cut your backboard rabbets, it's best to finish the cut at the bottom by hand. You want an easily controllable cut to avoid blowing through the pyramid. I used a chisel to score the extents, then chiseled out the waste coming in alternately from the side and top, to work my way down to full depth.

uncentered cutter for perfection before grooving the door pieces.)

Set the door pieces aside as you complete the sides.

On both ends, the upper and lower side rails get 1"-long tenons with ¼" shoulders. I marked the baselines with my cutting gauge (I find this cuts down on tear out at the visible shoulder line), then made some of the cheek cuts at the table saw with a dado stack raised to ¼", and some of them with a handsaw... once I realized that our sliding crosscut fence was slightly out of square. So I then cleaned up the table saw cuts with a shoulder plane, and the side panels got just a hair narrower. (I know better; one should always double-check setups!)

Test-fit the tenons in their mortises, and make any adjustments necessary. Once everything is closing up tightly and you have a good "press fit" (that is, you have to use a decent amount of hand pressure but no mallet to get the joint closed), pull the pieces apart and prep your panels.

I started with ⅝" stock, and after flattening one side of each walnut panel on the jointer and taking it to ⅜" with the powered planer, I switched to bench planes. We have a chipped planer knife that needs rotating and it's a bear to get rid of that track with just a smooth plane. So my No. 7 (jointer) got me within a few No. 4 (smooth) passes to the final thickness of ¼". (Plus, handplanes provide a good workout.)

Shelf-pin locations. Butt the mating pieces against one another, and make sure all four posts are aligned at the top. Now mark out the hole locations.

Test-fit the panels in the grooves. If they slide in fairly easily, you're home free. If they don't, take another pass or three with your smooth plane or random-orbit sander (ROS) and try again.

Once everything fits, cut the pieces to final size (remember to add ½" over-

FRONT

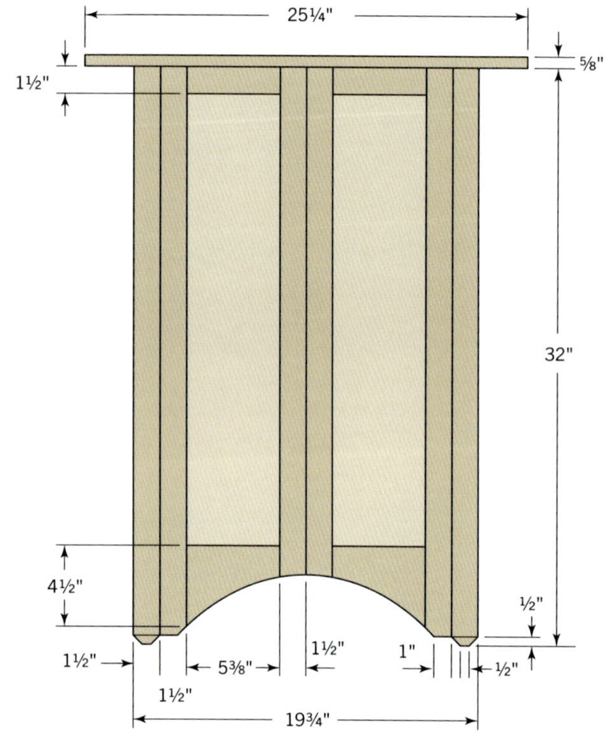

SECTION

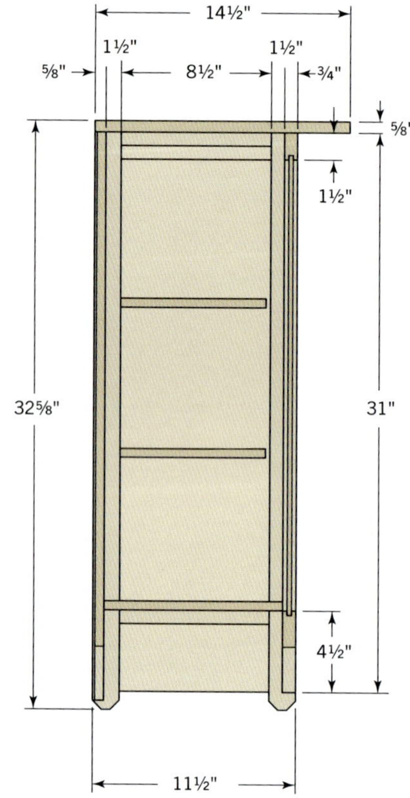

all to the length and width of what will show). I did this at the table saw (after resetting our crosscut fence to a perfect 90°).

Give everything a once over with your smooth plane (or ROS). It's easier to do it now than when everything is glued up—though you'll almost certainly have some surface clean-up to perform before finishing.

Now brush glue in the mortises and onto the tenons, slide the panels in place, and clamp everything up. (I keep a bucket of water nearby to clean up any glue squeeze-out, and I prefer liquid hide glue.)

While you're waiting for the glue to dry, cut the cleats to which the top and the bottom will be screwed. These fit between the posts and are glued flush with the interior top edges of the four rails on the side panels. This long-grain to long-grain glue joint is plenty strong enough for this application—promise.

Drill three countersunk clearance holes on the underside of each cleat, elongating them a little to allow for seasonal movement, then glue and clamp the cleats in place.

GET YOUR CASE TOGETHER

The sides are now complete, and you're ready to make a case out of this thing. For that, you'll need a nicely made bottom (and you should surface the lumber for the shelves at the same time).

The shelves fit between the posts, but the ½"-thick bottom is notched at all four corners to fit around the posts. The front edge acts as a stop for the doors, so it needs to be ¾" back from the post fronts; the back edge is even with the backboard rabbets. I cut the notches with a handsaw.

Groove on through. On the rails, the grooves run all the way through; on the door stiles, stop the cut in the mortise area.

Here's where the workholding is both critical and a little tricky; it doesn't hurt to have a friend help hold things in place as you align the bottom and screw it to the cleats. A thick backer board will also help.

With everything squared up and the bottom aligned exactly where you want it, drill pilot holes through the cleat clearance holes, then insert screws through the cleats and into the bottom.

After you've driven the screws on both ends of the bottom, check to see if things are still square. If they're a little out, don't fret; both the top and the backboards will help to bring things back to where you want them.

To assist, cut a scrap to the exact length of the opening. Flip the case on its top edges, position it as desired on the underside of your top, then place the scrap between the posts. Now screw

Cleats. After applying glue, clamp the cleats (or secure them with nails) to hold them in place as the glue dries. Either way, just make sure the countersunk holes are facing in the correct direction—toward the floor. (Here, you can also see the case bottom, with the corners notched to fit around the posts.)

CUT LIST & MATERIALS

	NO.	ITEM	DIMENSIONS (INCHES) T	W	L	MATERIAL	
CARCASE							
☐	4	Posts	1½	1½	32	Walnut	
☐	2	Top side rails	¾	1½	10½	Walnut	1" TBE*
☐	2	Bottom side rails	¾	4½	10½	Walnut	1" TBE*
☐	2	Side panels	¼	9	26	Walnut	
☐	4	Cleats	¾	¾	8½	Walnut	
☐	1	Bottom	½	9⅜	18¾	Walnut	
☐	1	Top	⅝	14½	25¼	Walnut	Live edge, use what you have
☐	1	Backboard	½	18¾	26	Pine	Assembled from 2–3 boards
☐	2	Shelves	½	8¼	18¾	Walnut	
DOORS							
☐	4	Stiles	¾	1½	31½	Walnut	
☐	2	Upper rails	¾	1½	7⅜	Material	1" TBE*
☐	2	Lower rails	¾	4½	7⅜	Walnut	1" TBE*
☐	2	Panels	¼	5⅞	26	Spalted beech	
SUPPLIES							
☐	4	Butt hinges	3/32	1½	2	Brass	

*TBE = tenon both ends

Bottoms up. Ensure the bottom is well clamped before driving screws through the cleats to secure it in place.

Topper. A scrap cut to the exact length of the opening helps you both to hold things in place and keep things square as you attach the top.

through the cleats and into the underside of the top.

Note that on my cabinet top, both the front and back edges are "live," so I aligned the case to the top by working off the ends.

I chose sugar pine for my backboards; the color will help reflect light inside the cabinet...plus I had a piece of pine wide enough that I needed only two panels for the backboards. I cut them a little over-wide, then joined them with a tongue and groove, which I dressed up with an 3⁄16" bead on the tongue panel. Not only does this create a nice shadow line (to help hide the gap between the two pieces), it mirrors the door opening at the front.

If you don't have a wide enough piece of wood for just two backboards, that's OK—you can piece it together from narrower tongue-and-grooved (or ship-lapped) stock.

Now cut the backboard panels to final width and fit them in their opening. This piece was built in the high humidity of an Ohio River Valley summer, so I spaced the center gap with two dimes (in winter, I use nickels).

Now comes the fun part—laying out the "perfect" curve (keep in mind that your perfect may differ from my perfect). I used a symmetric drawing bow because it's more precise and repeatable than my usual approach of tacking a thin strip of wood in place. The strap on the drawing bow retains the curve, which is important here. The same arc will be laid out and cut on the bottom of the doors; you need to be able to come back to it.

I marked points 1" in from the corners and tightened the bow until it was tangent to both points. But before settling on that curve, I showed the bow to the lower rails on the side panels. Why? The lower rails on the doors are the same width; I needed to make sure the same curve would leave a pleasing amount of the rail after waste removal.

Mark the curve, cut it at the bandsaw, then fair it with a spindle sander, spokeshaves, rasps, and files—whatever works for you.

Once you're satisfied with the way it looks and feels (touch will give you more feedback than looks, here), secure it in place with screws.

A NICELY FIGURED FRONT

Much of the visual impact of this cabinet depends on the doors—specifically, on the door panels. Building the doors is easy—it's grooves, mortises, and tenons, just as on the sides. And you should already have the grooves cut.

So cut the rails to length, cut the tenons, and fit them to their respective mortises.

Surface the door panel stock to ¼" thick. If you've chosen a spalted wood such as the beech I've used, take extra precautions with dust collection. Spalting is a result of fungi, and it can be particularly dangerous to your health.

Use the dry-fit doors as frames to locate the best-looking areas of your panels, then run a pencil around

My favorite molding plane. In just a few passes, a beading plane produces a lovely and crisp detail. Here, I'm using it to dress up the tongue side of my backboards.

Re-curve. A drawing bow allows you to retain a curve for as long as you need it (in this case, for the front and the back). When you're done, simply release the strap, and the bow returns to flat for storing.

the inside of each to mark out that good-looking rectangle. Mark a line ¼" out from each edge of the rectangles; that's your cut line.

Cut the first edge of each door panel at the bandsaw, then use a jointer or jointer plane to true the two edges. The rest of the cuts can then be made at the table saw.

Fit the panels to their doors and glue them up.

Now comes what was for me the most nerve-wracking moment in the entire project: cutting into the completed doors.

Butt the doors together, then trace the curve (I do hope you didn't reset your drawing bow!) on the bottom of the rails, starting 1" in on both edges. Before you make the cuts, check (again) to make sure the curve is below the bottom edge of the case bottom. That is, you need at least ¾"—more, really—remaining at the top center of the bottom rails. If the bottom shows it will a) look weird and ugly, and b) you won't be able to easily open the doors, because the doors have no handles; you slip your fingers behind the bottom rail to open them. Note that this cut will expose the edge of your tenons at the bottom of the doors; they'll still be plenty strong, and only the cats will notice.

The last task before final surface touch-ups and finishing is to fit the butt hinges. I always fit hinges by hand, using a marking knife to score the extents, then chisels and a small router plane to remove the waste. Typically, I'd say you could use a router and template for this work if you don't like the hand-tool approach—but in this case, you can't. The bottom hinge on each door is even with the bottom of the cabinet; a router simply won't fit.

Remove the hinges before finishing.

The finish is a sprayed coat of garnet shellac to warm up both the walnut and beech, followed by two coats of satin lacquer (with a light sanding between each). After the second coat of lacquer cured, I rubbed out the show surfaces with a brown paper bag, then reattached the hardware.

Because the back edge of the top extends past the backboards, I attached a French cleat that is proud of the back to hang the cabinet, with an offset block of equal thickness at the bottom (both are screwed to the rear posts and to the backboards).

The cabinet appears to float in front of the wall, which creates a nice shadow line at the back. It's also a practical solution to deal with hanging it on my 120-year-old wavy plaster walls—there's no need to scribe the posts to the wall for a flush fit.

Now I just have to design and build a similar table so this contemporary piece has company amidst all the Shaker.

Careful now. The doors are the most visible part of the cabinet. Cut carefully to ensure the apex of your curve meets at the middle.

MEDICINE CABINET

A slick technique makes the divided-light door a snap.

BY MEGAN FITZPATRICK

I once built a contemporary maple chimney cupboard to hold towels in my bathroom. Several years later, I decided it was time for a matching medicine cabinet—in large part because the house I recently bought has solid masonry walls, so I needed a nice-looking mirrored cabinet that can hang on the wall rather than be recessed.

So, using that cupboard as a starting point, along with a similar piece that hangs in a friend's bathroom, here's what I came up with: a simple-to-make maple medicine cabinet that takes its cues from Arts & Crafts, but with joinery and style details that give it contemporary appeal.

CASE CONSTRUCTION

When I initially modeled this cabinet in SketchUp, I used dovetails to join the carcase. But when it came time to build, I decided to use loose tenons instead. The resulting clean lines on the sides (no end grain) seem more in tune with an updated look, and loose tenons are plenty strong enough for this application.

But there is, of course, no reason you couldn't use dovetails (tails on the sides), or even dowel joints.

The Festool Domino, however, plus a trick for the divided-light glass door I picked up from David T. Smith (more on that later), allowed me to make this piece in about 12 hours of shop time.

After surfacing and cutting my four case pieces to size (note that the top and bottom are ⅝" narrower than the sides), I set up a dado stack on the table saw to cut ⅝"-deep x ½"-wide rabbets on the case sides to house the backboards.

I then laid out the shelf location on both side pieces so the shelf will be hidden behind the medial rail of the door, and lowered the blades to cut ⅝"-wide x ¼"-deep dados.

After checking to ensure the shelf dados lined up across the two side pieces, I laid out the locations of the Dominos.

To do this, butt the matching corners of the sides and top/bottom pieces together, make sure they're perfectly aligned on the front edges, then mark across the end grain of both pieces wherever you want a loose tenon (I decided on three at each corner—overkill, really). Separate the pieces, then carefully carry the lines around to the mating surfaces.

The Festool Domino, which is sort of a combination plunge-cut drill and biscuit joiner, can be adjusted for a tight mortise, a slightly less-tight mortise, and a loose mortise. At the front edge of every corner, I set the cutter for a tight mortise; for the other two, I changed to the medium mortise (which is but a millimeter or two wider). This ensures that at glue-up, the front edges are perfectly aligned, but there's just enough play in the middle and back mortises to get everything together easily.

Now cut the shelf to size and fit it to its dados. I like to plane underneath just at the ends if things are too tight. You're (hopefully) removing such a small amount of material that it's not noticeable to the naked eye.

The last task before gluing up the carcase is to lay out and drill shelf-pin holes for an adjustable shelf. I used a pair of dividers to walk off the hole locations about ⅝" off the front and rabbeted edges; the holes are spaced 1" on center. I decided (based on the size of some of my toiletries) on five possible shelf locations in the bottom section of the carcase. Your needs may vary.

I then used a drill press to drill ¼"-diameter x ⅜" deep holes.

Clean up the interior surfaces of the case, and the top and bottom of the shelf. I used a smoothing plane, though a random-orbit sander works perfectly well, too.

Efficient setup. I decided on ⅝"-thick backboards and a ⅝"-thick fixed shelf. That allowed me cut both the rabbet for the backboard (top) and the dado for the shelf (bottom) with one dado stack setup at the table saw. (I used a similar setup later to cut shiplap joints in the backboards.)

Domino layout. Make sure your lines match up and you can see them—layout (and good cuts) are key to a smooth glue-up.

Get a grip. Ignore that thing that looks like a handle at the back of the Festool Domino. If you grip there while plunging the tool, you're more likely to tip off horizontal. Concentrate on keeping the fence registered flat to the workpiece with your off hand; grip loosely at the base of the cord connection with your dominant hand and push forward.

Pinch. While cutting the mortises on the inside face of the sides, it's a bit more difficult to register the fence flat. Extend the support surface for the fence by butting the two sides together (which in this case provides an extra ¾" of bearing surface), and pinch the fence to the work with your off hand.

Level. A drill press makes quick and perfect vertical work of drilling the shelf-pin holes. But if you don't have a drill press, these can easily be drilled by hand—and there are dedicated shelf-pin bits that limit the depth and center the hole, available at any woodworking store.

Start the glue-up by painting glue on the loose tenons and inserting them into one of the side pieces (the tight-fitting tenons at the front edges will require some gentle persuasion), then attach the top and bottom. Add glue in the shelf dado and put the shelf in place, then glue the other side piece in place on the Dominos, and clamp across the width at the shelf, top, and bottom.

Note: Hide glue is more slippery than PVA—I find it makes glue-ups (and cleanup) easier.

BEADED BACKBOARDS

Set the carcase aside for the glue to dry, and move on to the backboards. Typically, I like painted backboards, but to my eye, that didn't work with this aesthetic. So I used the last of the maple I had in my stash (one of which was a cantankerous piece indeed) to cut a three-piece back with shiplapped joints. And because the table saw was still set up with a ⅝"-wide dado stack, the shiplaps are ⅝" wide. This build is all about efficiency.

But that doesn't mean I was willing to eschew a traditional bead on the edges—I'll be looking at the interior at least

Beaded. After planing the face of the backboards smooth, I cut a 3⁄16" bead where the shiplap joints meet. Note that the bead is cut on the full ⅝" thickness, not on the rabbeted surface of the mating piece.

Screwed. A screw at each corner (reamed slightly to allow for movement) will keep the back in place. Note the tearout... that would be the cantankerous board I mentioned. The front is smooth; that'll do.

twice every day—might as well enjoy the view.

As I noted earlier, the top and bottom of the carcase are narrower than the sides by the width of the backboard rabbet—that's to allow the backboards to run from top to bottom, so they can be secured to the back edges of the top and bottom.

I drilled countersinks and pilot holes—two at each corner of each of the three backboards, top and bottom, and used 1" x #8 screws (#6 would do, but I didn't have any at hand) to secure the backboards in place. I reamed slightly all but the four corner holes to allow the backboards to expand and contract with seasonal movement (not to mention the constantly fluctuating humidity of a bathroom).

I also used four screws on each of the two outside edges—be careful there; it's all too easy to poke through the side when drilling into the rabbet.

DIVIDED DOOR

The door is joined with one Domino at each corner, and one at each end of the medial rail. Again, take the time to get the layout right and register properly on your marks before making the cuts.

After the glue dries, rout a ½"-deep x ⅜"-wide rabbet on all four edges of each opening, and square the corners with a chisel.

Now comes the fun part—Smith's quick and clever method for dividing a door—it's most effective for flat muntins, which don't require coping. Each divider is simply two pieces of wood—a front piece, which I'm calling the muntin, and a back bar (or retainer strip) that sits in the rabbet.

First, use dividers to lay out the approximate locations of the two muntins in the rabbet, top and bottom (it's approximate because the final locations will shift a tad in relation to the width of your muntin stock).

ELEVATION

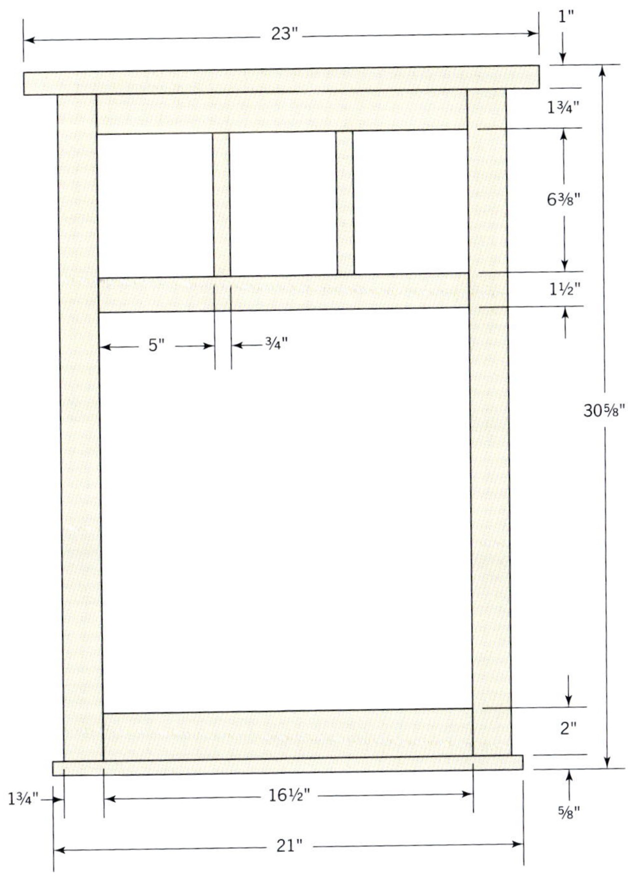

PROFILE

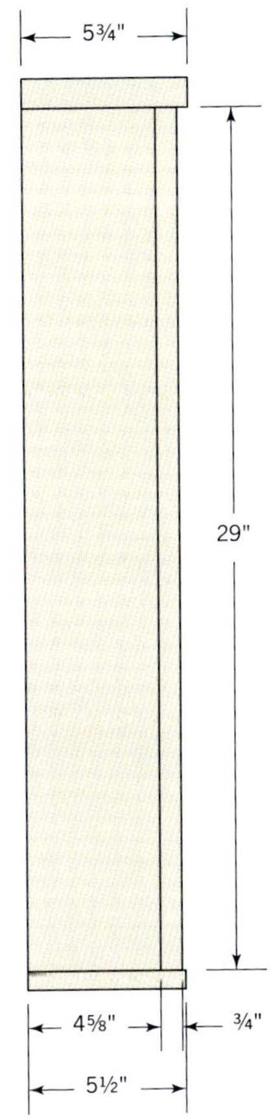

Now prepare enough ¼"-thick stock for the two back bars, plus a piece or two extra, just in case. The width should match (or be just a little proud) of the depth of the rabbet—so in this case, ½".

Cut two pieces just a hair overlong, then shoot the length for a perfect fit, and mark a centerline at the top and bottom of each piece.

With the back bars dry-fit, cut the ¼"-thick stock for the muntins (those need to match the thickness of the frame in front of the rabbets).

Again you're going for a perfect fit—any gaps will be noticeable.

Now dry-fit the muntins behind the back bars and shift things as needed to get three equal-sized openings. Mark that location on the top and bottom of the opening so you can easily line up the centerline on the back bars.

Put a dab of glue in the rabbet, then pin the back bars in place.

Flip the door, put a thin bead of glue on the front of the back bar, and center the muntin on it. This long-grain to long-grain glue-up will be plenty strong enough to hold the glass in place.

TOP & BOTTOM

My original design had a coved top to match my chimney cupboard; that shifted in my head to a bevel on the underside as I put together the carcase.

So, I cut the top to size, then placed it on top of the carcase to determine where the bevel should terminate. But

Rout it out. A rabbeting bit and router makes quick (if messy and loud) work of cutting rabbets, but you do have to square the corners with a chisel...or cut your glass with round corners.

CUT LIST & MATERIALS

	NO.	ITEM	DIMENSIONS (INCHES) T	W	L	MATERIAL	COMMENTS
CARCASE							
☐	2	Sides	3/4	4 5/8	29	Maple	
☐	2	Carcase top & bottom	3/4	4	18 1/2	Maple	
☐	1	Shelf	5/8	4	19	Maple	
☐	1	Top	1	5 3/4	23	Maple	
☐	1	Bottom	5/8	5 1/2	21	Maple	
☐	3	Backboards	5/8	7 1/8	29	Maple	Shiplap, trim to fit
DOOR							
☐	2	Stiles	3/4	1 3/4	29	Maple	
☐	1	Top rail	3/4	1 3/4	16 1/2	Maple	
☐	1	Medial rail	3/4	1 1/2	16 1/2	Maple	
☐	1	Bottom rail	3/4	2	16 1/2	Maple	
☐	2	Back bars	1/4	1/2	7 1/4	Maple	Oversized, shoot to fit
☐	2	Muntins	1/4	3/4	6 1/2	Maple	Oversized, shoot to fit
☐	1	Glazing strips	3/8	1/4	164	Maple	Cut lengths to fit
SUPPLIES							
☐	2	Butt hinges	3/32	1 3/4	2	Satin nickel	
☐	2	Round ring pull	1/2	1 5/16	1 1/2	Satin nickel	
☐	1	Mirror	1/8	17	17 7/8	Mirror	Cut to fit opening
☐	3	Glass panels	1/8	5 1/2	6 7/8	Clear glass	Cut to fit openings

then I stepped back to have a better overall look at the thing, and realized I liked how the square edges pick up the lines of the flat muntins.

So square edges it is for me—but don't hesitate to add a bevel or molded edge if you like; that would lighten the cabinet both in looks and actual weight (and a cove would give it a more traditional look).

I finish-planed the top and bottom, then simply glued them in place and clamped them to dry. There's a lot of glue surface; they aren't going anywhere.

I then fit the door with a reveal of about 1/16" at the top and bottom, and installed the pull and butt hinges. (See "Butt Hinge Installation" on p. 140 if you need help with that process.) I prefer silver over gold tones, so I opted for a satin nickel finish on my hinges and pull; I think dark antique, or even black iron, would also look nice. Remove the hardware for finishing.

FINISH DETAILS

Ideally, I'd have finish-planed the door pieces before assembly...but I got over-eager to move forward on the build and forgot. So that meant sanding. I started with 80 grit and worked up to 180 grit.

Press fit. You want the back bars (or retainer strips) to fit tightly top to bottom in the rabbet. A shooting plane will help you sneak up on the perfect fit.

Pin it. Put a dab of glue in the rabbet, then pin the strips in place. Note: I'm merely holding the muntin in place here with my fingers.

Glue it. Glue each muntin to its retainer strip, then secure spring clamps at the top and bottom of each muntin to hold them in place until the glue sets.

Glazed. Thin strips of maple hold the glass in place and provide a clean look on the interior.

With all visible-to-my-naked-eyes scratches removed, I used a rag dampened with alcohol both to remove the dust, and so I could more easily see if there were any machine marks or plane tracks that I missed. (There is little more disheartening in woodworking than putting on a coat of finish only to have it call attention to a faulty surface.)

The finish is simply three sprayed coats of pre-catalyzed lacquer (which I'll keep a close eye on and recoat if necessary—polyurethane would be better for a bathroom, but I don't like the look). After the final coat dried, I rubbed down all the surfaces (OK—maybe I skipped the back of the backboards) with a gray Scotch-Brite pad (or 00 steel wool) to remove dust nibs and to make the surface feel silky-smooth.

But wait—you still have to install the glass.

Both the mirror and the three clear glass panels are ⅛" thick (I had them cut at a local glass and paint store), and are housed in ½"-deep x ⅜"-wide rabbets. So that means you'll need glazing strips no more than ⅜" x ⅜". And while it doesn't matter a great deal on the mirrored glass because they won't show through, for the clear glass you'll want to make sure no strip peeks into the opening—so check that before you pin them in place.

The strips are simply butt-jointed and secured with 23-gauge pins. You could use glazing points or silicone to hold the glass in place, but I prefer the clean look of the strips, and it doesn't take much extra time to make and install them.

Before reinstalling the door, screw a French cleat to the top of the carcase (secured at both long edges and in a slightly elongated hole in the middle) and a strip of equal thickness at the bottom of the case; that will keep it at 90° to the wall when you hang it.

Put the hinges back in, hang the door, and reinstall the pull.

The door on mine hangs closed, so I didn't add a latch of any kind. If in the future I decide one is needed, I'll simply inset a small rare-earth magnet at the front edge of the side's interior face, right where the screw for the ring pull hits the case.

Now you're ready to hang the piece (secure the other half of the cleat to two studs), step back, and admire your work—and yourself in the mirror.

BUTT HINGE INSTALLATION

1. Locate. Hinges are typically installed in this type of build with the leaves registering off the door rails. So I use a combination square to line things up. I always start with the door, not the case.

2. Mark. Hold the hinge firmly in place with your off hand, and use a marking knife to score around the edges. A series of light cuts will be more effective than one deep cut. Now set a cutting gauge to the exact thickness of the leaf and mark the mortise depth. (I've penciled in the lines here for ease of viewing.)

3. Chop. Make a series of cuts in the waste with a chisel, and use the tool to deepen the edges you marked with your knife (bevel facing into the waste, of course).

4. Clean. Drop the router plane blade in the baseline, then tighten it. A few passes with the plane will lift out the waste and smooth the bottom of the mortise. (You can also set the router plane to the thickness of the hinge leaf, and use the plane to mark the bottom of the mortise, instead of a cutting gauge.)

5. Screw holes. Drop the hinge in its mortise and mark the screw-hole locations, then drill. Be careful to not drill through the stile.

6. Screws. Screw the hinges in place; a little wax on the threads will make it easier. (I typically install only the top and bottom screws at this time; it saves time when removing the hardware before applying a finish.)

7. Mark the carcase. Now fit the door to its opening, with the desired reveal shimmed at the top and bottom. Hold the door firmly in place. Register the flat of the marking knife off the barrel of the hinge and make a nick. Do the same for the other hinge(s). I always mark the bottom of the leaf. It's a habit that keeps me from cutting the mortise on the wrong side of my mark (that's more of a fear for me when there's also a middle hinge).

8. Narrow material. The process for the hinge mortises on the sides is the same as for the door—except that, if you want to retain the small amount of wood behind the hinge mortise, clamp a piece behind it for support as you're chopping. If you don't, it will certainly tear out. There is, however, no shame in simply cutting the mortise across the full thickness of the side.

EIGHT COMMON HINGES

Every door needs a hinge—find out which hinges to use, the advantages of each type, and how to install them.

BY NANCY HILLER

Wherever there's a door, there must be hinges—and just as there's a galaxy of door types, there is a variety of hinges and modes of installation. Even when we narrow the field to those used in furniture and built-ins (as distinct from entry doors or gates designed for cattle), the options are many. Here, we'll describe the uses and installation of several common varieties.

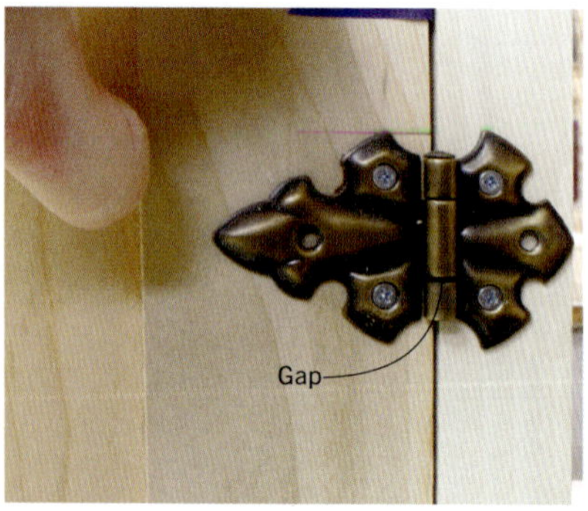

Vertical play. This hinge had a lot of vertical play. The larger gap below the center section of the barrel is from my holding the door up. Compensate for this play when inserting the screws, or the door will sag.

Inexpensive shims. The door is resting on a pair of pennies that act as shims; another pair of shims is taped to the hinge stile to create the desired gap between the door and the frame.

BUTTERFLY/APPLIED HINGES

Surface-mounted hinges are decorative, often having strong period associations—especially with built-ins from the early 20th century—and are simple to install. There are two main varieties: inset or half-overlay doors.

First, determine the position of the hinges on the door. Many butterfly hinges have sloppy-fitting pins that allow for more movement than is desirable. (Stay tuned—I'll address this later.)

Set one flap of the hinge on the door, positioned so the barrel is just under halfway onto the door's hinge stile. Leaving the barrel a little less than halfway over the edge of the door will create a small gap between the door and the cabinet side or face frame.

Drill for two screws in each hinge using a Vix bit (a specialty bit that drills holes centered on a hinge's mounting holes), then insert two steel screws of the same size as those you will use in your final fitting. Leave the third hole alone in case you need to adjust the position of the hinge.

Set the door in its opening on shims. For this demonstration I used pennies. I also taped pennies to the hinge stile to create a gap of the same width. Hold the door steady with one hand and drill two holes in each hinge with the other. Then insert screws and check the fit.

If there's too much play in the barrel, adjust the fit by moving a screw to the third hole and pulling or pushing the door up or down until it hangs as you want it.

Once the door is fitted, mark the holes for final hanging, remove the hinges, sand, and finish. Then insert the finish screws.

You can use the same method for half-overlay doors; just insert the coins under the ledge of the rabbet.

BUTT HINGES

Butt hinges are common on furniture and built-ins. Although they come in a variety of sizes and types, most are installed according to a basic sequence of steps.

The simplest form of butt hinge is the surface-mounted variety that does not require a mortise. They're so easy to install that we won't cover them here.

Traditional butt hinges come in two types: swaged and non-swaged. Whether or not a hinge is swaged can be figured by how it sits when fully opened—a swaged hinge has a gap (as seen below) when closed.

The most common type of hinge we used in England was the fixed-pin non-swaged butt, which we mortised into the door stile only (I'll describe an application where this is called for later). In the United States, we mortise these half into the door and half into the cabinet, so this is the technique I'll describe in detail.

Non-swaged. Hinges that are not swaged have their leaves in line with the barrel.

Swaged. A swaged hinge has leaves that are bent inward toward the center of the barrel.

Fixed-Pin, Non-Swaged Butt Hinges (Mortised into Door & Carcase)

Determine the position of the hinges. Next, square the line for the end of the hinge around to the face of the hinge stile. Lay each hinge in place and scribe the location of the opposite end of the leaf with a marking knife.

Set a marking gauge for the width of the mortise and scribe the edge of the hinge stile.

If you have two marking gauges, set a second to the mortise depth: Hold the hinge leaf against the gauge's reference face and adjust until the pin (or cutting wheel) is just shy of the pin at the center of the hinge barrel.

Now that you can see the mortise depth, scribe a line across the door face from each end of the hinge.

Use a wide chisel to chop out the waste. Begin with a series of cuts across the grain. Stay a bit away from each end to prevent marring those shoulders. You'll pare them later.

Next, use your chisel bevel up to pare the waste. After you've removed the bulk of the chips, pare to the baseline, staying away from the bit of waste left at each end.

Hold your chisel vertical with the bevel facing the inside of the mortise and pare away the bit of waste at each end, going down to the baseline. Finish up by paring that waste down to the line. Check the fit, and pare more material away if necessary.

Use temporary screws while fitting doors. Just be sure you use screws that are the same size or slightly smaller than those you'll use for the final installation. Here I used #6 x ⅝" Twinfast screws, which are easy to insert and remove. Use a Vix bit to drill holes for the two outside screws in each hinge. Leave the third hole alone. If you need to adjust the position of the hinge, you can drill a fresh hole later.

Mark the width. To lay out the mortise width, set a marking gauge from the edge of the hinge leaves to the center of the pin in the middle of the barrel.

Scribe the width. Mark this width between the outer lines.

Scribe the thickness. Set the gauge to just under half the thickness of the barrel. However much your pin (or cutting wheel) is short of the hinge pin's center will be half the gap you'll have around the door.

Easy does it. When cutting across the grain to break up the waste, stop just short of the baseline to avoid going too deep.

Waste away. Pare away the waste, taking extra care as you place your chisel tip in the gauged line to remove the final shavings.

Put in place. With the door shimmed in place, mark the hinge positions on the cabinet frame using a knife. I also circle my knife marks with pencil to make them easier to see.

Set the door in its opening, shimming as necessary to get the gap you desire at the bottom. (I used a pair of pennies.) Mark the top and bottom corner of each hinge with a knife.

Turn the cabinet on its side to finish the mortise layout.

Repeat the steps above to lay out the hinge mortises on the cabinet. When you've finished cutting the mortises, test the fit.

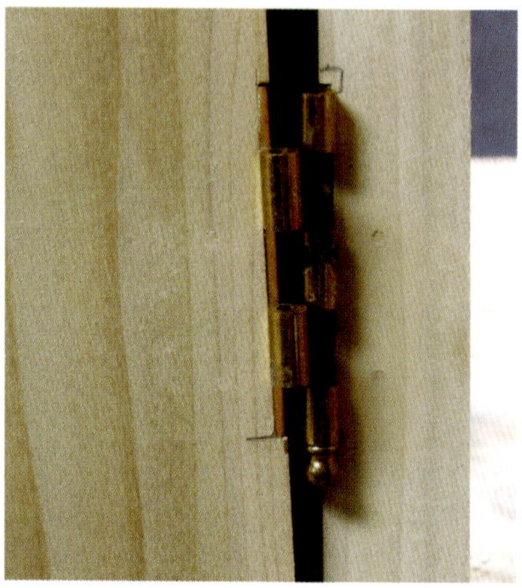

Sliding home. Place the door so that the hinge leaves fit together, then drop in the pins.

Leaf, no barrel. To lay out the width of a swaged, loose-pin hinge mortise, set your gauge to just the width of each leaf.

Loose-Pin, Swaged Ball-Tip Hinges (Mortised into Door & Carcase)

The process of installing loose-pin hinges is similar to that just described, but with a few differences. Loose-pin hinges tend to be swaged and have a different barrel position on a door. Whereas fixed-pin, non-swaged hinges are mortised so that the outer edge of the door stile hits the barrel of the hinge approximately at its center, loose-pin, swaged hinges are installed with the entire barrel clear of the door's edge; this way you can tap the pin's finial gently from below with a screwdriver and mallet to remove it.

Full depth. The swaged loose-pin hinge is mortised flush with the wood, so set your gauge to the thickness of one leaf.

Revealing. Fixed-pin, non-swaged butts will be let into the door with the cabinet-side leaf protruding by the amount of your desired gap around the door, so I am setting the gauge shy of the barrel's thickness by about 1⁄32".

Because the pins are removable, it's important to install the hinges so that the pin drops down into the barrel. For example, ball-tip hinges have one fixed finial that goes on the bottom; the pin with the other finial fixed to its end should drop in from above.

Start by setting a marking gauge to the mortise width. In this case, though, the mortise will be only as wide as a single leaf, because the barrel will protrude from the cabinet.

Mark the mortise width. Set the other gauge to the thickness of the mortise—in this case, the thickness of a single hinge leaf.

Scribe the thickness on the door and repeat the processes as described above to complete the layouts.

When you have screwed the first leaf into each mortise, lay the door in its opening on shims and transfer the hinge positions onto the cabinet as in the first example and cut the mortises. Now you're ready to try the fit.

Fixed-Pin, Non-Swaged Butt Hinges (Mortised Only into the Door)

Some jobs call for non-swaged butt hinges to be mortised fully into the door. Although it's uncommon in the United States, this is a method used often in England. It saves labor but is arguably less durable, especially for heavy doors, because the entire weight of the door is borne by the screws. For example, I once built an Arts & Crafts sideboard that calls for this method. Because the doors are set back about 1" from the face of the cabinet, they would not work if they were mortised halfway into the cabinet as well as the door.

This method is basically the same as the first butt joint method, except

INSET, HALF-OVERLAY & OVERLAY DOORS

We reference a number of cabinetmaker's terms concerning three different configurations of doors relative to their carcase—inset, half-overlay, and overlay. Before we dive into each hinge, it's worth indicating what these terms mean. (Note: Other hinge types can be used for these applications—this sidebar deals only with those described here.)

Inset doors lie within the cabinet. This style can be used with both frameless and face-frame cabinets. Traditionally, furniture with inset doors would use butt or butterfly hinges (though other varieties such as strap or rat-tail hinges are common in older furniture). European hinges may be used for inset doors in modern cabinets.

Half-overlay (also called half-inset) doors have rabbets that allow half the door's thickness to be enclosed inside the carcase. These doors can be hung on butterfly or European hinges. Because there is no visible gap around the door, these hinges make for easy fitting.

Overlay doors hang proud of the face frame (or frameless opening). European hinges are commonly used for this application.

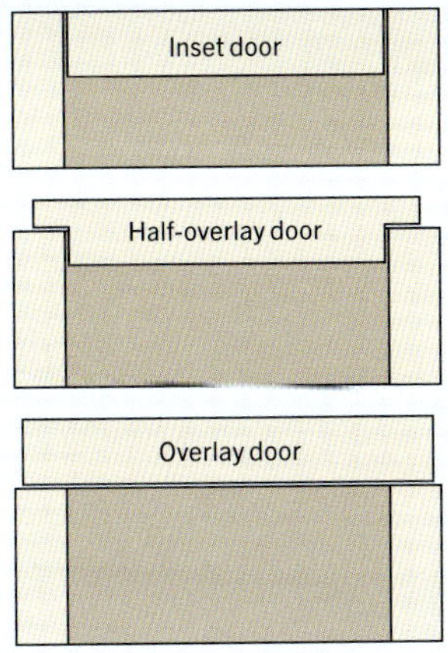

that the marking gauge for the mortise thickness should be set to just under the thickness of the entire barrel: If you want a gap around the door of, for example, 1⁄32", you should set the gauge for the thickness of the barrel minus 1⁄32".

Mark out and cut the mortise as in the first example (p. 143).

To transfer the hinge positions to the cabinet, set the door in its opening on shims, but mark with a sharp pencil instead of a knife. Remove the door and mark the leaf width onto the cabinet side using a marking gauge; this will guide you in aligning the door from front to back.

Because the hinges have fixed pins, hanging the doors in this method is a little awkward: You have to hold the door with one hand while drilling the hinge holes with the other. It can take more than one try. I find it best to drill the first hole in the upper hinge, then insert a screw in the top hole. I hold the door steady and close it so I can check whether the face of the door is flush with the face of the cabinet. If it's proud, I use a bradawl to mark the center of the next hole down a little farther back, remove the door, drill a hole in that new spot, and try again. When the face of the door is where it should be, I drill the bottom-most hole in the lower hinge, insert a screw, and repeat. Once you have a screw in the top and bottom hinge, you should be home free.

PIANO HINGES

Piano hinges provide continuous support for doors and large box lids. They can be cut to length with a hacksaw, then mounted directly to the edge of a door or lid without mortising.

Piano hinges are made with a series of holes along their length. Sometimes a few holes are elongated to allow you to adjust the position of the door. This works when you use the entire length of the hinge, but many jobs call for cutting the hinge to a custom length. In these cases the result will be neater if you center the holes on the door or lid you're fitting.

After you have inserted enough screws in the door side to hold the hinge in position, hold the hinged door

On center. The center of the door's length is marked in pencil and the piano hinge is positioned so that its center hole falls over that line.

HINGE REFERENCE GUIDE

HINGE TYPE	GOOD FOR	NOTES ON INSTALLATION & USAGE
Butterfly/applied hinges	Inset or half-overlay doors and period applications, such as matching original hardware.	Easy to install. Your face frame and door stile must be wide enough to accommodate leaves. These hinges can have some slop.
Fixed-pin, non-swaged butt hinges (mortised in door & carcase)	Inset doors for high-quality traditional furniture and built-ins.	Require precision installation. Order hinges that will leave at least 3⁄32" of wood in thickness at the back of the mortise.
Fixed-pin, non-swaged butt hinges (mortised only into the door)	Cabinets where the door is recessed relative to its surrounding framework.	Fully recessed doors can only open 90º and can't support heavy loads.
Loose-pin, swaged ball-tip hinges (mortised in door & carcase)	Inset doors for traditional furniture and built-ins, especially early 20th-century styles.	Being able to remove the door makes this type of hinge ideal for easy installation and fitting. Especially good for heavy or awkward applications.
Piano hinges	Long doors or lids requiring full-length support.	Easy to install, and can be trimmed to fit.
European hinges (inset doors/frameless cabinets)	Built-in cabinets with inset doors that don't need to match an existing style.	Easy to install and adjust, and hidden when the door is fully closed.
European hinges (full-overlay doors/frameless cabinets)	Overlay door applications, when paired with a mounting plate.	The same as above—and varying mounting plates allow differing amounts of overlay.
European hinges (face-frame cabinets)	Cabinets where the hinge-side face frame stile protrudes into the door cavity.	Can also be used, in a pinch, with a cabinet where the stiles don't protrude, with a thin applied strip.

Careful work. A Vix bit will work on piano hinges, though their leaves are on the thin side, offering less meat for the countersink on the bit to land—so make sure the bit registers properly on the hinge's hole.

against the cabinet in its final position. The barrel should protrude by exactly the same amount on the cabinet as it does on the door (or not protrude at all, if that's how you fitted the hinge on the door). Drill a hole at one end and insert a screw, then repeat at the other. If you need to adjust the door a little to either side to even up the hinge relative to the cabinet, remove a screw, move the hinge, drill, and insert a screw into the hole nearest the first one. When you're happy with the fit, drill and insert the rest of the screws.

EUROPEAN HINGES

European hinges come in a dizzying variety, each designed to work in different situations. Most consist of two parts—a hinge and a mounting plate—though those designed for cabinets with face frames have an integral mounting plate. Depending on which combination of hinge and mounting plate you use, these hinges can work with doors that are inset, half-overlay (sometimes, confusingly, called "half-inset"), or full-overlay, in which the full thickness of the door is proud of the cabinet face.

And there are more—lots more—variations: A full-overlay door may overlay the cabinet face by ¼" or 1¼", depending on the mounting plate you use. Doors can open 95° or as much as 165°. They can be free-closing (these do not hold themselves closed but require a catch) or self-closing. Some of these hinges are even available with a soft-close feature that shuts the door for you once you give it a gentle push.

Despite the huge variety, all of these hinges have the same pattern for drilling the hinge cup mortise in the door: a hole drilled to the depth of the cup (about ½") with a 35 mm Forstner bit. The edge of the hole should be ⅛" away from the door stile edge.

First decide where you want the hinges. Keep in mind any fixed shelves or other interior features that may be in the way. These hinges and mounting plates occupy more interior cabinet space than many other types.

If you are using a drill press, set the depth to stop at the thickness of the hinge cup. Then drill for the screws using a #5 Vix bit. Insert the screws.

After this initial work is where the method of installation diverges, depending on your style of European hinge and installation plan.

European Hinges on Inset Doors/ Frameless Cabinets

Although this method works for frameless cabinets, it works just as well for those with face frames, provided that the face frames do not protrude into the door opening. And, even if the face frame does protrude into the opening, you can still use this method if you shim out the mounting plate so that it lies in line with the face frame's inside edge.

Most doors will need some adjustment after installation. All European hinges offer easy vertical adjustment, and most now allow you to adjust the fit laterally as well as in and out.

European Hinges on Full-Overlay Doors/Frameless Cabinets

The method for overlay doors is similar to the method for inset doors, though you need to buy a mounting plate for the amount of overlay you desire (that is, the amount of the cabinet that is covered by the door). On page 148 I used a zero-height plate with a straight-arm hinge for a ¾" overlay. Once again, this can be used on cabinets with face frames.

Set and shim the door in place as it will hang. Then, follow the steps used to install and adjust the inset doors.

European Hinges on Face-Frame Cabinets

Face frame hinges are made for applications where a face frame protrudes into the door opening. These hinges have mounting plates that simply fit over the edge of a ¾"-thick face frame. (If your face frame is thicker, you can notch the frame.) Drill for the hinge cup and screws, then attach the hinge to the door.

Big holes. First drill the holes for the hinge cups using a 35 mm Forstner bit. A drill press with a fence enhances accuracy. The edge of the hole should be ⅛" from the edge of the hinge stile.

Little holes. As with the other hinges, I use a Vix bit to drill the mounting screw holes once the larger holes for the hinge cups have been drilled. Alignment is easy, as the hinge sits in the larger holes for the hinge cups.

Open back. It's easiest to install these hinges before you affix the cabinet back. Simply set the door in its opening, shim with a wedge to hold it in place, and drill the holes from the cabinet interior.

Looks familiar. As with the European hinge for inset applications, the overlay version for frameless cabinets involves a hinge and a mounting plate.

Slip fit. Face frame hinges differ from other European hinges in that the mounting plate on the cabinet side fits over the edge of the face frame.

Fix it in post. Clearly this door at top right needs some work. No worries—European hinges are made for just this type of situation. Screws on the hinge will move the door in and out, laterally or vertically. After this adjustment (shown at bottom right), the reveal around the door is even.

TAKEAWAY LESSONS

There are many ways to hang a door—and these are just a few of the common hinges. In reality, here's how to narrow the choices:

■ Will your doors be inset or overlay?

■ Should the hinge be hidden from view? If so, consider European hinges.

■ Are you matching an existing door? Existing door hardware will guide you.

■ What is your budget? A 4' section of piano hinge will be much cheaper than hanging a 4' door with three quality reproduction ball-tip butts.

■ How much adjustability would you like? Mortised butt hinges give you virtually none; European hinges offer adjustability in three planes.

■ If your shop setup is minimal, consider a piano hinge, which requires a drill and screwdriver. If you have a traditional hand tool setup, go for fully mortised butts.

■ The ultimate decider: What is available?

Finally, of course, don't forget those pennies.

TOOLS AND SUPPLIES

Visit your local woodworking store or look online for these brands mentioned in the book.

Ball & Ball (reproduction hardware) ballandball.com

Briwax (waxes, polishes) briwax.com

Brusso (hinges and hardware) brusso.com

Clapham's Beeswax Products Ltd. (wax furniture polish) claphams.com

Festool Dominos (joiner, joinery) www.festoolusa.com

General Finishes (stains, finishes) generalfinishes.com

Horton Brasses, Inc. (furniture nails, reproduction hardware) horton-brasses.com

kaDON (taiko byo tacks) kadon.com

Olympic (stains, paints) www.olympic.com

Scotch-Brite (cleaning and scrubbing pads) www.scotch-brite.com

Tremont Nail Co. (brads) tremontnail.com

Van Dyke's Restorers (tacks) vandykes.com

Watco (stains) www.rustoleum.com

Whitechapel Ltd. (reproduction hardware) whitechapel-ltd.com

CONTRIBUTORS

Black, Ty: "Six-Board Chest" (variation builder, p. 60)

Brown, Ted: "Krenov-Style Memories Box" (author, p. 23)

Favorite, Mary Jane: "Country Tool & Toy Chest" (illustrator, p. 51)

Fitzpatrick, Megan: "Contemporary Cabinet" (author, p. 126)
"Country Tool & Toy Chest" (author, p. 51)
"Medicine Cabinet" (author/photographer, p. 134)
"Shaker Blanket Chest" (author, p. 81)

Henriksen, Timothy. "Six Board Chest" (variation builder, p. 60)

Hiller, Nancy: "Eight Common Hinges" (author, p. 141)

Huey, Glen D.: "A Simple Sea Chest" (author, p. 66)
"Inlaid (Bible?) Box" (author/photographer, p. 14)

Lang, Robert W.: "Inlaid (Bible?) Box" (illustrator, p. 14)
"Stacking Bookcases" (author, p. 54)

Parrish, Al: "Inlaid (Bible?) Box" (lead photographer, p. 14)
"Japanese Sliding-Lid Box" (lead photographer, p. 36)
"Medicine Cabinet" (lead photographer, p. 134)
"Rediscover a Shaker Classic" (lead photographer, p. 29)

Pessell, Dan: "Japanese Sliding-Lid Box" (illustrator, p. 36)
"Medicine Cabinet" (illustrator, p. 134)
"Rediscover a Shaker Classic" (illustrator, p. 29)

Pierce, Kerry: "Pleasant Hill Classic Cupboard" (author/illustrator, p. 118)

Rogowski, Gary: "Illusion Cabinet" (author, p. 111)
"Jasmine Jewelry Box" (author, p. 7)

Schwarz, Christopher: "Danish Modern Campaign Chest" (author, p. 72)
"Japanese Sliding-Lid Box" (author/photographer, p. 36)
"Old Plane Birdhouse" (author, p. 47)
"Pleasant Hill Firewood Box" (author, p. 57)
"Roy Underhill's Nail Cabinet" (author, p. 104)
"Shaker Wall Cupboard" (author, p. 101)
"Six-Board Chest" (author, p. 60)

Spagnuolo, Marc: "Greene & Greene-Style Blanket Chest" (author, p. 93)

Stanton, Chad: "Stacking Tool Caddy" (author, p. 41)

Weber, Don: "Traveling Toolbox" (author, p. 88)

Wilson, John: "Rediscover a Shaker Classic" (author/photographer, p. 29)

INDEX

Publisher: Paul McGahren
Editorial Director: Kerri Grzybicki
Design & Layout: Clare Finney

Cedar Lane Press
PO Box 5424
Lancaster, PA 17606-5424

Paperback ISBN: 978-1-950934-73-7
ePub ISBN: 978-1-950934-74-4

Library of Congress Control Number: 2021945060

Printed in the United States of America
10 9 8 7 6 5 4 3 2 1

To learn more about Cedar Lane Press books, or to find a retailer near you, email Info@CedarLanePress.com or visit us at www.CedarLanePress.com.